D1422294

LUCINESRI

A CHILD LOST IN
AN ALIEN WORLD

K . PHELPS

authorHOUSE®

AuthorHouse™ UK
1663 Liberty Drive
Bloomington, IN 47403 USA
www.authorhouse.co.uk
Phone: 0800.197.4150

© 2017 K.Phelps. All rights reserved.

No part of this book may be reproduced, stored in a retrieval system, or transmitted by any means without the written permission of the author.

Published by AuthorHouse 02/23/2018

ISBN: 978-1-5462-8220-4 (sc)
ISBN: 978-1-5462-8221-1 (hc)
ISBN: 978-1-5462-8219-8 (e)

Library of Congress Control Number: 2018901825

Print information available on the last page.

Any people depicted in stock imagery provided by Thinkstock are models, and such images are being used for illustrative purposes only. Certain stock imagery © Thinkstock.

This book is printed on acid-free paper.

Because of the dynamic nature of the Internet, any web addresses or links contained in this book may have changed since publication and may no longer be valid. The views expressed in this work are solely those of the author and do not necessarily reflect the views of the publisher, and the publisher hereby disclaims any responsibility for them.

Lucinesri

Looking through all the research we'd collected through the years I felt a hot sweat prickled onto my forehead. We were running out of time. A selected team of teachers, engineers, doctors, nurses, architects, pharmaceutical scientists, carpenters, farmers etc. are here frantically trying to help. I fear our efforts are in vain. Our secret mission coming to its deadline and I was solely responsible for all these lives. I made them a promise to do all I could and there I was, almost out of resources, almost out of patience and almost out of time.

We've all spent the last few years creating our vessel, building it, preparing it and filling it with necessities, all in preparation for the end.

Everyone here, every single, hardworking soul had sworn to secrecy and signed their promise on paper not to allow officials know our plan. They wanted to save the rich and influential, not what we considered important. Not the ones who actually had something to give in a time where money wouldn't be of value.

Unfortunately, we lived in a world where, if you wanted to be saved, you needed to pay. For some reason, cotton based paper with ink on was the most valuable thing you could own. We didn't believe that. So we were going to try and save as many as we could. We just needed to find a place to go.

I remember desperately searching through the data on the screens and paper in front of me, checking coordinates and rushing to our telescope to search, hoping upon hoping with each glance, I'd find our salvation.

After hours, I felt the last of my hope draining away, sweat making me feel grubby as it did everyone else. I felt a failure. I couldn't give up. I had too many lives depending on me and I couldn't give up on them, on everything we've worked for over the years. I especially couldn't let her down, my Lucinda. I lost her at the beginning of this mission. I missed her dearly each and every day, even to this day, I think about her. That's why we named the vessel after her. New Hope (N.H Lucinda).

I tiredly checked another coordinate before stumbling over to the telescope. A flash. Could it be? I adjusted the settings. The image cleared. This could be it. I felt the hope reignite. My heart raced. The more I looked the more I knew. Certain in my heart. Certain in every molecule of my being. As the image grew clearer. I could tear myself away. It was perfect. The only place we could go. The one place that had been dismissed as the 'new Earth'. Dismissed due to 'not producing oxygen' but an oxygen substitute, known as Oxygecine. Now it was our 'New Home'. We either stayed here and died or we risked it to save ourselves.

I ran from the room, shouting and raving about the discovery. Everyone cheered and I saw it, they spark in their eyes, long since faded with time, back for good. The atmosphere changed. Everyone working harder than ever to finish the last few checks and fixes to the N.H.L. we were ready the next day.

I lead the way to open the ship and allow all my team on board like a proud father. They looked worried. I couldn't blame them. We were about to attempt to leave behind everything we'd ever known for a chance we didn't even know would definitely work. Of course we knew the chances, we'd calculated them thousands of times. There was a risk with every alternative. One thing that was 100% certain was we'd be dead within a week if we stayed.

I gave a speech. Although I was afraid myself, I was in charge. I had to comfort them.

"We have worked for years for this. You have worked through sweat, tears, frustration and desperation for this, and now the moment of truth has arrived. Come with me and I will try my best to get you there. We must stick together, support each other and stay calm. Panicking will get us nowhere now. There is nothing left for us here. Let's go and find the life we've been working for. Come with me and we will find ourselves. A new home. A new kingdom. A new start. A new history. For us, for our future children and grandchildren. Let's do it. For all of us."

I was surprised at the round of applause I received for my speech. I'm not much of a public speaker.

We all took our seats.

Silence. Then, countdown. We braced ourselves as the rocket took off, pinned against our seats as we were propelled vertically into the air, out of the atmosphere we'd called home all our lives. No turning back now.

I felt my stomach threaten to come out of my mouth. I still remember the sound of the wind and it rolled over the ship's aerodynamic design. A low, loud rumble as it tried to slow us down. It seemed to stop as we left the atmosphere but I knew we were actually still going. The co-ordinates locked I heard the team cheer. We were on our way.

After travelling for a few months, we were finally approaching our destination. It wasn't easy. We got restless, some people we at each other's throats. Now all was forgotten as we pulled on our spacesuits and made our final preparations to land. Checks were called, followed by the confirmation that they'd been carried out and all was ready.

We strapped in. once again we braced ourselves for the pull into the planet's gravitational pull.

And there we were, pinned to our seats as we raced towards the surface, bright, fresh, green islands with large areas of water. Very similar to Earth. I heard a few screams escape the mouths of the crew as we missed the landing, sliding across the land as speed until we came to a crashing stop against what seemed to be a form of large hill.

We waited, checking everyone was ok before they looked at me for answers. I took a deep breath and made my way to the door.

Months had led to this moment. Now it was here I was scared. We could die as soon as this door was open. We didn't know if the air was breathable. No was the time to find out.

My shaky hand opened the door with a clank, the suck of the oxygen as it escaped through the newly opened gaps around the door. I pushed.

Light blinded me as my sight adjusted to the new world that lay before me. It was all so fresh and green. Tall, strange trees filled my line of vision every which way I turned.

Trickle. What's that? Water? Yes, a small water fall further up from where we landed. We'd have to do tests to see if it was drinkable but we had water. Everything was untouched and pure and everything we'd ever wanted. I couldn't take enough of the scenery in. my sight eventually, landed back to my crew, waiting, watching me. I knew what I had to do. I reached for the clasp around my helmet. The moment of truth.

My heart was pounding in my ears as I slowly pulled the helmet off of my head, holding my breath. Now or never. I inhaled, prepared for it to burn my lungs. Dissolve me insides and kill me...but it didn't, I inhaled again and again as we all celebrated. Leaving our suits behind to begin our new lives.

I was honoured when they asked me to be King and name our new home. I name it after my inspiration, Lucinesri...

Extract from The New Home, in the words of King Wolf, 2367

250 years later...

I see the little figure run up the hallway in front of me, her braids streaming behind her, making a game out the task at hand. Bed time is always a game.

'I'm going to get you.' I teased as I fake run after her. Her laughter fills the hallway making echoes' off the high ceilings.

She runs through the open door of the bathroom. I follow in still teasing that I'm going to get her. I walk in, look round. I look behind the bath, in the gap under the draws beneath the sink. She isn't there. 'Where has she gone?' I ask myself.

All of a sudden I feel a tiny pair of hands grab my waist and I scream. Half behind the bathroom door, there she is, in hysterics about frightening her mother. I can't help but laugh with her.

'Right you,' I say getting down to her height, 'time to brush those pearly whites.' I grin.

She runs past me to the sink, pulling her steps in front of it so she can reach. I song our Teeth Brushing Song, just as I do every night. It's the only way to get her to brush them.

Mr bristles is going to clean up your teeth, clean up your teeth, clean up your teeth

Mr bristles is going to clean up your teeth, until they're sparkling clean.

Simple but effective. It makes her laugh. Her laughter is the best noise ever to me. It's infectious, if she's happy, it makes me happy.

I take in her miniature features as I wipe toothpaste from her mouth. Her bright grey blue eyes with a faint patch of brown in her right one. Her round cheeks, her full lips and her very long eyelashes which would make anyone envious.

'Right sweetheart, go choose a book then.' I didn't even need to guess which one she chose, she always had the same. I could recite it word for word. The Adventures of Banjo the Starman, even make the voices for each character as I tell her. A bold, bright voice for the hero and a low, slow voice for the villain. I repeated how the villain 'borrowed' Banjo's spaceship to try and steel the stars and how Banjo cleverly defeated him in a simple way that kids could relate to all the while it had its secret meaning about how you ask first before using something that doesn't belong to you. All the time I had her under one arm co-cuddling as I story-told.

Afterwards, she lead down and I pulled her cherry blossom covered duvet up to her chin and kissed her goodnight, making sure she had her three-eyed purple furry monster. She can't sleep without it.

I turned out the light and closed the door before making a beeline for my room, next door.

'ADELINA!' I was startled awake so badly I was shaking, my focus wasn't connecting. 'Come quick! It's Andromeda!' that was it. I was awake. I was focused. I half fell out of bed in my hurry, sliding across the floor. What time was it? It's still dark. My heart is still racing from being woken.

I get out the door, turn left towards Lyra's room and all the helpers are there crowded around the door. One sees me and makes her way over to me. Her hands on my shoulders she tell me not to get in there, desperation in her voice.

'Why? What's happened?' I'm scared now. I pushed them out the way and step into her room.

Air. A cold breeze hits me. The moonlight fills the room, the only other light being the nightlight out the corner of my eye. The window isn't open though. It's broken.

'Adelina, you shouldn't be in here. I've called the police. Let's get you out of here.' My father enters, placing his hands gently on my arms. The police? Why? My heads darts to the bed. The covers are messed up and pulled back. She isn't. Where is she? Panic. Fear.

'Where is she? WHERE IS SHE?!' I scream. I continue to scream. I get guided out of the room. What was that on the floor? Glass? It looked black. Who would do this? I continue to scream. I don't care what's on the floor.

My duvet feels like a weight on my shoulders. I don't know when I stopped screaming.

I feel numb and pained all at the same time.

My eyes hurt. I've been crying.

Someone is holding out a cup of tea to me. I can't make out who, my unbrushed hair bordering my face blocks them from my view. I shake my head letting them know I don't want it but the action sets me off again and hot tears burn my cheeks.

Every part of my body feels like it physically hurts, especially my chest, which feels like my heart has been ripped from my chest as my mind silently wishes that it's all a one horrible nightmare and I'll wake up at any moment.

I don't though. It carries on. People walk around me in a blur. I can't hear what's being asked of me.

Everything hurts.

Time passes and my tears have subsided. At least, for now. I press my hot head against the cool glass, watching the people walk by down below, going about their daily routine. Their accustomed, safe, repetitive lives. Anger rises within my chest. How dare they? How can the go about their lives like nothing has happened? How can they be laughing and chatting and going to work while my life has been torn apart?

The window is more like a wall. Happiness and sunshine out there and misery and darkness in here.

'Adelina?' though my name was mentioned gently, the sudden break in my thoughts made me jump.

I turn my head, saying nothing. He doesn't ask if I'm ok. I think my eyes say it all. Red, bloodshot, tired and sore. He looks at me like he wishes he could take the pain away, even goes to touch my face before retracting his hand, 'these men need to talk to you now.'

I focus my gaze on the officers' standing behind him. I hadn't even noticed them prior.

I know they entered through the secret back entrance to the castle. No one can know about this. I can't talk about it. I can't turn to anyone for support. This is my own.

'Yes?' I try to sound brave but the quiver in my voice gives me away.

'Your Highness-'

'Don't!' I interrupt. 'It's Adelina. No, Your Highness. No, Princess and no Majesty!' my voice rises as I speak, struggling to maintain my calmness. My title isn't relevant here. I'm a mother who is grieving. Nothing more at this precise moment in time.

'Hey. Calm down, its ok' my father tries to comfort me. It most definitely is not 'ok' it is far from ok. This is the worst moment of my life and he thinks its 'ok'! I don't say this though. My rational side tells me he's only trying to help and the officers are too. They're doing their job.

One of the officers clears his throat. 'We need you to make your statement.'

'I'll leave you to it...' my father stands up, squeezes my shoulder to reassure me before making his way to the pale blue doors and exiting my room. I'm hurt. The time I need him most and he leaves. He might only be the other side of the door but he might as well be on another planet.

I half-heartedly wave my hand in the direction of two nearby chairs from my custom made dresser. A 16th birthday present from my father 7 years ago. They make a noise similar to nails on a chalkboard across my laminate floor. I don't flinch. Once comfy, they ask their questions. Where was I last night between 7pm and 7am? Who had access? Do I know anyone who would want to hurt me? Etc. I answer in monotone not even looking at them.

Then they ask: 'can you please gives us your versions of events please?'

All of a sudden the chest pain in back and fresh tears fill my eyes giving me a headache. One of them hands me a tissue as I try my hardest to regain my breathing rhythm so I can talk. Only as I take the tissue do I look at them properly and take in their features.

One was human, the other was Scillian, a reptile like humanoid with larger scales atop his head, making him look like he was wearing some form of head wear.

'At 7 I got her ready for bed.' I say slowly, trying to remember every detail. 'I put her in her pyjamas, brushed her hair. 2 braids, she likes 2 braids. Brushed her teeth and let her choose a book. The Adventures of Banjo the Starman. Her favourite. She has it every night.' I paused, was I missing something? It seemed like I did more last night. How can a whole evening be summed up in a few sentences? Especially when it's so important. 'Then I tucked her in. Told her I loved her. Closed her curtains and left her. She goes to sleep on her own. She's a good sleeper. I closed her door. I went to my room. I stayed there for the rest of the evening and went to sleep about 10.'

I'm sure there's more. I ran through it all again in my head. That's everything. So why does it all feel so unhelpful?

'And that's it?' asked the Scillian sceptically.

'Yes' I reply, still unsure.

'Nothing else happened?'

'No' what was he trying to ask?

'What did you do during the time you left your daughter's room until you say you went to sleep at 10?' the hum asked checking his notes as to what I has said.

'I read. I wrote in my diary. I made my to-do list. Things I do every night.' I feel panic rise. Did they know something I didn't? Had I forgotten something so important about my evening I now looked suspicious? I would never put her in harm.

'Miss Lune. Can you think of anyone who would want to get back at you or your father enough to think that taking your daughter-'

'Her name is Andromeda!' I shout. Angry. She is a Being. Just like the rest of us. She has her own identity for crying out loud.

'Sorry' the human muttered sheepishly before continuing. 'Enough to think Andromeda would be leverage or a punishment to either of you?'

'no.' I reply, 'but I can't speak for my father.'

The officers look at each other and nod. 'Thank you Miss Lune, that's all for now. We'll let you know if we find anything.' They promised.

Yes, I'm a Princess. I hate it. Everyone who works in the palace goes out of their way to make me happy, they don't even challenge me. They never have. Boring.

I wouldn't have any enemies, to the best of my knowledge, who would want to hurt me in this way. My father made sure I wasn't raised in the public eye. Hiring teachers to educate me and giving me my privacy. Our kingdom has only ever seen my baby picture announcing my arrival into our world and I wanted the same for my child.

Lucinesri is my home.

I was educated heavily in the history of Earth, in my 5x great grandfather's race to save 100s of people. He made sure we welcomed the visitors that arrived after us, allowing them into society. I'm proud of that don't get me wrong. I just don't feel like I could be Queen. Despite being prepared to take over leadership of this planet, I don't feel like I could handle the responsibility. Yes there are leaders of the other islands in this world but I'd be the one in charge. Making all the difficult decisions. Having to think and lead the way my ancestor intended. No pressure.

My ancestor ruled on equality. Forging laws that allowed other species seeking refuge to live alongside humans, believing that we could find peace by learning about the way each lived, sharing our skills and by never repeating the mistakes Earth made by trying to repent differences. My relative lived by the quote: don't destroy what we fear. Educate and learn. Lack of knowledge makes us fearful.

In doing so, making sure that no child was left without a family, allowing those who couldn't have children, either through lack of fertility or same-sex or interspecies relationships not allowing a spawn to survive for reasons unknown, but mainly from vastly anatomically different genetic structures. I remember my teacher passionately telling me this historical victory. She was adopted by parents of different species.

For that, I live by and am so proud to be a Lucinerian.

I can hear the investigators chatting away in the next room, I hate them for it. My mind scolded them for it. *'Just get on with it and find my baby!'* more tears. I thought I was all cried out.

I decide to shower. I knew that there'd be a meeting with the Lunar Fleet soon. I'd know then what was going to happen with the investigation. What I could do to help. There's no way this would be allowed to be public knowledge. It'd be too risky.

I ran the water fast and hot, just so I could feel something other than this pain. This feeling that made me feel like I'd rather feel anything else but this. This burning from my heat making everything ache. The pain I can't erased with painkillers. The worse pain I could possibly believe existed. I cried more in the shower. *'Where was she? Is she ok? Is she hurt? Does she know we're trying to find her?'* so many questions. All made me feel useless.

The Meeting of the Lunar Fleet

I practically flew down the long hallway to the secure meeting room high in the tower. I needed answers and I needed those hours ago.

The hall seemed never ending, as if the hallway was elongating with every step I took as I raced towards the door emblazoned with our crest depicting a supernova.

I tried my best to look presentable. I would've gone in my pyjamas except I know that with any given chance Commander Costello will use any excuse to not take me seriously and dismiss me, even given the circumstances.

The large, cold door is heavier than usual. I push as hard as I can, past the guards in full armour and Nysa guns, ones that can fire multiple red pellets that once a capsule hits you can burn you from the inside out, as frantic chatter fills my ears. Large windows allow the August sun stream in, making the dark grey room. I make my way to the head of a large table, where my father and Commander Costello, who towers over my father, are in talks over the information in the files lying before them.

I can hear my own breathing, it's like I'm floating through the room. The voices sounding muffled around me, getting quieter and quieter as I reached the end, the only voice I needed to hear was the one who was going to tell me what was to happen next and what I needed to do to help.

I caught Commander Costello turn his head in my direction, his yellow eyes filled with disgust as I walked in their direction before checking that my father's attention is otherwise occupied.

'You took your time.' He snarled, his sharp teeth on show as he spoke.

'Not in the mood.' And I'm not, normally I would have had some smart remark to retort. Not today. Just like any other day I couldn't give less of a damn about him.

He gives a low growl, making the gill like slits in his face flare and his silver-blue sebum face flash red. As he's turning away as my stomach ties itself up in knots as my patience wears even thinner.

Costello is a hard man, former soldier. Great at his job and being Bonytriggerdi, his survival skills in water proved invaluable but, for some reason, dislikes me. He'll brown nose my father no end, even pretend to be my friend. He thinks I got my job as Second in Command, because of my status and not my hard work. My 'Queen in training' regime helped me to get my job by teaching me how to make the decisions needed. I worked hard. He refuses to see it. He's egotistical, mean and will push his soldiers.

How will he talk to me when I'm Queen?

I take my seat as my father calls the meeting to order. Costello puts a smile on his face as he pulls his chair, purely for my father's benefit. He is revelling in my pain. What did I do to him? Multiple chairs scrapping across the floor reminds me of fingernails across a blackboard. I shudder.

The chatter stops immediately as we all sat on tender hooks, eager to hear what the plan was and what our roles would be.

I can't help but tap my fingers on the desk in anticipation while my father wastes yet more time in arranging his damn papers. Like it's important right this second. How long is it going to take? What am I meant to do? What do they know?! TELL ME!

'Ok' he says quietly before clearing his throat, 'I'm sure we are all aware of why we are here…and why we need to keep it between the people in this room. It must not be discussed with people who are not involved. It is to be handled carefully and with consideration.'

He sounds…old. His voice is filled with a sadness I don't recall him displaying before.

'For those who may not be informed,' he continues, 'just a few hours ago, my granddaughter, Adelina's child, was taken from her bed.' He looked my way before continuing, checking I was ok. I don't need this right now. Every second that passes was another second me precious girl was away from me, probably scared and alone. Costello, lets out a low, throaty growl at me to stop tapping my fingers. I comply. This time. The last thing I needed today was him being annoyed with me. Quickly as a flash I hid my hand under my arm.

'We have evidence which leads us to believe a known, convicted, criminal is responsible.' I sit up like a dog, my sense pricked. Who? Who is it?

Before us the table lights up projecting a hologram of the suspect. A thuggish oaf of a man appeared before me, the pale blue hologram light illuminating everyone's faces.

The picture depicts a moderately overweight middle aged human with a dark tan and a scar by his eye. I fixate on this image, unable to take my eyes away. Anger and disgust boils form the pit of my stomach making me feel nauseated. I have to find him.

He continues to talk, something about the evidence they found, I think he said feathers, something black, I don't know. What are they talking about? I can't focus. I can't connect back to the room. Something about...other evidence...what? I try to hear what's being said but it's muffled. Snap back, Lina-now!

'Where do we find him?' I interrupt.

'Well, uh, we need to still check the evidence- 'my father answers, thrown by my interruption.

'What more evidence is there? He can be placed in the room. He has a record. Where do we find him?!' I can feel myself getting emotional again, weighted breaths escaping from my chest. I can't believe this.

'I know this is difficult but try to calm down Adelina.' My father says quietly to me. He looks genuinely shocked by my reaction as the blue light casts a shadow over every crevice on his face. Am I supposed to be composed? Contained? Calm? As a princess is expected to act? Well, news flash! I'm a MOTHER! That's how I'm acting!

'I can't 'calm down' this man has my child.'

'I know and we need to go about this with thorough thought through plans and procedure. Also...we don't know where he is...' he trails off

'What?!'

'We're working on it, love.' He offers.

'So that's the plan? Sit back and wait until they find him? Not good enough. Give me the file. I'll find him myself.'

'Maybe, we should have this conversation in private, your Highness.' Costello offers in his low voice, raising from his chair.

'Good idea.'

Reluctantly, I follow them both. The Commander's armour clinking with each step. The office door clicks shuts as I flop myself down on the chair. A file lands on the desk in front of me.

'What's this?' I ask picking it up.

'It's the suspects file.' My father tells me. I instantly open it upon being informed of this news. 'His name is Rigel Allard.' He tells me. I read the information. Name: Rigel. Age: 46 Criminal History: Robbery, Theft And Battery. Last known address: Vulcadon...the capital-here! Where we are right now. He's here, we can find Lyra.

'He lives in the capital-we can find him!' I exclaim filled with hope.

'It's not that easy.' Costello says. He almost sounds sad. 'My men have already followed the lead. The property is empty. It has been for some time.'

A dead end? No! I'm frustrated and hurting and I'm doing nothing. Don't they get that? I'm meant to protect her and look after her yet, here I am, when she needs me the most, doing nothing.

'What do we do, dad?' I ask on the verge of tears again as I return the file to the desk.

'The only thing we can. We have to search for him. The members of the Fleet in that room have been searching since early this morning. We'll have investigators go over the reports from his arrests. Search his history. Try to find a link or a connection to a place or Being. We'll find Lyra.' my father reassures me by coming to my side and finally hugging me. I'm not convinced that he's convinced by this plan though. I finally feel I can relax for a moment, leaning against the man who raised me alone (with the help of the castle staff of course) and all of a sudden I'm back to 5 years old afraid of the monster under the bed. I feel weak. Numb and in pain at the same time. With all our resources and technology and there's so little we can do. I'm such a failure. I couldn't protect her. I feel so hopeless.

Beep. Beep. Costello's communication screen comes through with a message. We don't break from our hug.

'Sir...we have a lead.' Costello carefully interrupts our father-daughter supportive moment. My father breaks the hug before I'm ready and I have to pull myself back to being a grown up and wiping my own tears as Costello listens intensely to the voice in his ear piece. Each ear piece is specially adapted to fit the individual's ear. After a few seconds he returns his attention to us. 'They found a connection between Allard and a former petty criminal. He works in the mechanics sector of Vulcadon. Let's go.' He orders reopening the door behind him, allowing us past. Everyone is back to doing whatever they were doing before the meeting was called to order. Armour clinking, their bots sounding heavier than they are. Loud chatting making the room feel overwhelming. We make our way back to the table but a soldier runs over to meet us, obviously eager to share this discovery.

'The suspect is 24 year old, Jacob Noble. Research suggests he teamed up with Rigel Allard in his teens and was threatened with a Secure Training Centre sentence when his links with Allard arose but he has no further charges since. He trained in the Minors Military Unit, where he learned mechanics.' The soldier rambled, handing the new file to the Commander.

'Well done soldier.' Costello praised. He'd have never praised me. 'Send me his work location ASAP.' He ordered as we all headed towards the door.

'I don't believe questioning him will be helpful, Sir.' The soldier replied, worried. We all glared at him. The only link to Lyra and he was refusing orders.

'What do you mean, soldier?' my father asked gravely.

'Well, uh, he was meant to join the Fleet but was demoted to mechanics after refusing to give evidence against Allard. Questioning him will be useless. He won't talk about him.'

Another brick wall. Any glimmer of hope keeps being taken away. I feel my stomach fall away. I can't breathe and I can't believe it. Something needs to be done.

Costello sighs. 'What else is there?' he asks the soldier in an expectant manner. He wasn't asking what the next move was. He was waiting for more information.

'There has to be *something*.' I say quietly, mostly to myself. I look around. Researchers frantic at their computers, investigators examining the hologram of the suspect and the files of the lead. It felt like chaos. Soldiers, known for their composer and formality are here, seemingly losing their minds. 'We need a plan.' I say louder.

'Well, obviously Lune, what do you think we're doing?' Costello scoffs.

'No. I mean an actual plan of action.' The room is quieter. Beings listening to, what could be, another argument between me and Costello. 'Everyone is here, running around, frantic and –don't get me wrong I'm grateful- we're not getting anywhere.' I pause thinking and muttering to myself.

'Rigel isn't about. Evidence says he's the suspect. The lead won't talk to officials...' I stop. Lightbulb moment! 'That's it!' everyone looks confused. 'He won't talk to officials about Rigel. What if he didn't know he was talking to an official?'

'An undercover agent.' Costello sums up.

'Yes! Someone needs to get him talking, get the evidence we need without him realising.'

'I don't know, Adelina. We don't know anything about this man.' My father voiced his concerns.

'Maybe not.' I turned to my father. 'But we don't have any other leads and in my opinion, we don't have any other options. He might know where Rigel is. We find Rigel, we find Lyra. That's all I care about.'

'There's still other evidence we need to process.' Costello sided with my father. 'But she's right, it won't be a quick way around the problem, could take a few days-a week at least, but it's the only plan we have. I say we follow it.' I was shocked. He never agrees with me. 'We need a list of everyone involved in this case and what their roles are. We need to know who we can spare for undercover work, remember as King Callisto said, no one outside this room is to be involved.'

'Yes, Sir' the soldier answered before running off to get the required list.

'Uh, dad?' I say as him and Costello make their way to the table again. 'What's my role in the case? What am I doing?'

Costello whirls round stopping me in my tracks. 'I don't think that's very wise, Princess. You're too emotionally involved in the case. You're fragile state could ruin the case and put the young Princess at risk.'

'At risk? You really think I'd put my own child at risk?!' I don't believe this man. 'Don't you get it, the most precious thing in the world has been taken from me and so far I haven't been able to do anything! I'm supposed to protect her! I'm supposed to look after her! I need to be involved...I need to help. I can't be useless.' I try to hold back the tears that are blurring my vision but they threaten to fall.

'Maybe, the Commander is right, love.' My father says it like he's trying to spare my feelings. The kidnapper didn't consider my feelings when he took my baby, why should anyone think of them now? 'Everything you're feeling is still raw, that puts you-and this case- at risk of falling through, along with every lead we have. I want to bring Lyra home. We need to trust our Fleet with her safe return like we trust them to protect this planet.'

My shoulders fall, defeated. They're right. I can't risk her getting hurt, even if it means I take a step back. Sometimes knowing when to fight for your child is also knowing when to take a step back. I nod to let them know I agree as the tears, once again, fall. 'I better go back home.' I say quietly turning towards the crest emblazoned doors again.

I take my time walking to the door. I don't have anywhere to be. It's just empty at home. Every steps feels heavy. I wrap my arms around myself in an attempt to self-comfort. I don't think it works. Still in this room full of Beings and I'm so alone.

'Commander.' I hear the eager soldier trying to get his attention. I hear the crinkle of paper. I hear Costello's low 'I'm annoyed' growl. An exasperated sigh from someone.

'We don't have much of a choice now.' Costello tells my father.

'But she's not stable enough.' The King protests.

'You said it yourself, no one outside this room is to be brought in.'

'Can't we bring someone in this once?' he pleads.

'No, it could compromise everything.' Costello counters.

Another exasperated sigh. 'Ok.' He sounds drained. I put my hand up to the door to push it open.

'Adelina!' I turn to see my father beckoning me over. What now? I just got told that I shouldn't be part of the case. They have a grave look on their faces when I reach them.

'We have a bit of a problem.' Father tells me.

'Add it to the list.' I says miserably.

'We don't have enough people on the case to spare anyone to go undercover.' He continues ignoring my remark. 'Against everything we've just said it's come to our attention that... we might actually need you help after all.' He doesn't sound confident.

'What about compromising the case?' I ask echoing their previous words.

'We can't allow anyone outside to be involved. We've made the decision to risk it.' Costello isn't confident either. I don't blame him. I am too emotionally involved but now I have a newly ignited hope starting to ease the pain in my chest but I refuse to get excited.

Suddenly a thought dawns on me, I haven't been trained for this. I feel my eyes widen at this realisation. I can't think of that now. I take a deep breathe.

'What do I need to do?' I ask trying to sound confident. The Commander holds out his arms to direct me.

'You need to talk to him, befriend him. Gain his trust before even attempting to phish the information out of him.' He informs me. We stop at a door. I realise it's the weapons room. Did I miss something? How dangerous is this guy? The security code gets typed in along with an identity card swipe on the lock before the reinforced doors slide open.

Before me, rows of dark strong shelves appear each stacked with different weapons in different sizes and with different uses. Some fired pellets like Nysa guns. Some fired lasers that can cut straight through you and others were hand held, easy to hide ones that all guards had for extra defence against attack. We traipsed past rows of these weapons until we came to a small hand held device called a Cariopius, a device with multiple uses. One end has a retractable mini cutlass. The other had a mini Bio Orb, a light activated by shaking a bioluminescent slime excreted from the Deep Blue Distinctus. Luckily the slime is able to be collected without even touching the creature. It has a clip so a Being can secure their selves to a rope for safety a recording and tracking device that can only be activated by the user.

'Take this.' Costello orders before swiftly turning back and exiting the store room. 'We don't know this man. You know as much about him as the rest of us. We'll keep looking for Rigel and any known associates here. Keep us updated. We are relying on you now.'

No pressure. At least, I'm not concerned about the pressure from them. The pressure I put on myself will be far greater.

A thought strikes me 'wait, I'm not a mechanic.'

'You'll have to work as a Spare, learn the skill. We'll arrange it so he teaches you.'

A Spare? Of course I should've realised. Lucinesri has a great system where if you lose a job and none are available in the sectors in which you're qualified, you become a Spare. An apprentice if you will. You get put into a new sector and learn a new skill from scratch. It means everyone does their fair share and no one is left without a job and all jobs are filled. It also means if someone is ill there's no end of Beings who can fill in.

The door closes and locks itself behind us. I hold the Cariopius in my hand, examining it. Small, handy, black in colour except for the pale stone which the light shone through allowing the light to cover a bigger surface area. The crest is engraved along its side. I take a deep breath and pocket it.

'I better go pack.'

Back in my room, the sun shines through, making it warm and welcoming but to me it feels empty. Janus helps me pack. She's one of the 'Friends of the Palace', the respectful way my father likes to call our staff. Why not? They have done so much more than 'help'. They helped raise me. They're family.

'I'm scared, Janus.' I confide.

'I'm not surprised, lovey.' She tells me, smiley sweetly at me showing her triangular teeth. Like the police officer from this morning, she is Scillian. I try to smile back but the corners of my mouth don't make it. She gazes at me sympathetically. 'Oh, darling.' She mothers, drawing me in for a hug. 'I think you're being so brave through this. I can't imagine how you must be feeling.'

I know she's trying to help, but it doesn't. She's concerned. She's seen Lyra grow since the day I bought her home as a tiny new born.

'Let's not waste any more time, shall we? Let's get packed.' She says it almost like I'm going on holiday. Silently I thank her for her acknowledgement of time. I turn to get a few pairs of trousers from my wardrobe. I see on the side a book. Not just any book. The Adventures of Banjo the Starman. I pick it up like it's the most fragile thing in the world. My breath gets caught in my throat. I hand it to Janus. She looks wary.

'Are you sure, Adelina?'

'I need to. It's her favourite. If-when I find her...' I lose my words but Janus understands and carefully places it in my suitcase. We pack the rest of my necessities in silence.

'Thank you.' I say quietly to her before making my way towards the castles' entrance where my transport would be waiting.

Spare

The warm air rushes over my face, filling my lungs. The sun is hot but I'm walking towards the Mechanics Centre in my knit jumper. I feel numb as the world rushes around me, families going about their daily business as the hover crafts and practicing Fleet jets zoom overhead. My nerves turned and tied into knots on the way over here.

The tall building almost sparkled in the sun as it shone onto the solar energy frame covering the entire frame of the building as it soaked up the beams and transferred it into energy just like it did for all the other buildings. It meant no coal mines or oil rigs had to be forged like it was on Earth.

A tall figure approached me and the craft driver, one of the soldiers from the meeting room entrusted with ensuring my safe arrival. As the figure grew closer I felt as though I was shrinking and everything loomed over me, intimidating me.

His appearance came into view. Large crest comb on his head. Large, multiple slits between his four dark eyes. A Gallina.

The sun momentarily blinded me as it caught his medals that stated his rank. Colonel. The man in charge here. Costello said he'd have someone ring ahead.

'The new recruit I presumed.' His tone was warm as he held out his webbed hand in welcome. I politely shake his hand.

'Yes. That's me' I manage a small smile.

'Follow me then.' He smiles warmly before turning to the one that transported me here. 'Thank you, solider.' They salute each other before I follow the Colonel into the Centre. 'I'm Colonel Stevens. I've been informed by a member of the Spare Sector that you've been made redundant. Sorry to hear about that. Where one door closes another opens. We've been in need of a new recruit.'

I agree with the redundancy story. I assume this is meant to be the back story Costello created for me. A good one. Simple, few questions. I go along with it. He leads me towards the door shrouded on arches that created a shelter over the door. I pulled the handle of my suitcase, dragging it behind me.

I follow, almost sprinting to keep up with him. Tall, echoing walls surround me as we enter the reception. Voices and a ringing noise filled my ears, almost deafening me in its process of reverberating of the surfaces. We approached some sliding doors and we enter a large floating pod that made me feel even smaller than I already was. Everything seems so big while I feel small. It's quite daunting and intimidating.

In silence we take the lift to the 10th floor as the magnets inside the walls of the building and the pod reacted together sending us smoothly upwards.

'The Being I'm putting you with is one of our best mechanics, so be assured you'll learn a lot from him.' I think Colonel Stevens is trying to reassure me so I politely nod my head in acknowledgment.

Although it was probably only 2 minutes, it felt a lot longer being in that pod so I was relieved when the doors opened onto the 10th floor.

I continued to follow him down the corridor, suitcase in tow, in the side of the building that's in the shade so it's instantly cooler. We pass door after door and making momentary eye contact with craft drivers coming into land as they pass the windows. With all my emotions drained I feel exhausted as if we'd been walking forever by the time we reach the last door of the corridor. A quick scan of his ID and the iron door swiftly opens revealing a large room. The room is bright. A small kitchen area directly in front of me alongside 3 large hydraulic jacks for air craft repairs, one jack occupied with a Fleet Fighter Jet. Along the far wall is a reinforced steel shutters to allow craft enter and exit. Along each jack were wheeled toolboxes, no doubt filled with every nut, bolt and power tool imaginable.

I'd always expected garages like this to be dusty and dull but, to my surprise, it's so clean. Pristine in fact. Dazed, I mindlessly take a few steps as I take in my surroundings. Seemingly ignoring my detachedness, the Colonel slides confidently into the room ahead of me and clears his throat.

'Now where is he?' he asks himself. 'He should be here.' His attention turns to me. 'My apologies miss...' I hadn't given him a name, panic spikes. Quick think.

'Mond.' I say the first word that comes to mind that means the same as my real last name. I know I can't give my real name but I also want to keep my identity in a place 100% different from what I know. 'Lina Mond.' I say dryly and trying to act casual. I look out the window and mull over the day's events.

'NOBLE!' ugh, what now? I hear Stevens' voice boom. I'm trying to reconnect the wires on the top of this blasted air draft. No matter what I've tried I can't get it to start.

I clamber to my feet, grab the frame of the hydraulic lift, climbing down the outside before letting go and dropping to the floor, straightening myself up before Stevens could turn around. He jumped out of his skin and I almost a laugh.

'What d'you want?' I asked. I see he's brought a girl with him. I look at her. Her eyes are red. She's been crying. The redness makes the green of her eyes stand out brightly. She doesn't look at me. She's sad and distant. She's about the same age as me. Whatever has upset her so much is where she is mentally. Poor thing. She's pretty though. She's short, 5'2" at the most, average size. Her hair is pulled into a lose ponytail as her hands rest on her suitcase. She is wearing a navy jumper, probably 2 sizes too big. She must be boiling in this summer heat. I feel my heart rise in my chest with empathy.

'There you are.' Stevens begins. 'I have a surprise for you.' This means I won't like it. My eyes dart to the girl still looking out the window. 'This is Miss Mond.' Hearing her name she turns her attention to us. 'She's a new Spare. She's been assigned to you.'

'I told you I didn't want a Spare after what happened to Leo.' I tell him annoyed.

'Now, Noble, don't be rude. You know you don't get a choice. Spares get assigned to whoever is available.' Stevens replies in his chipper way, as usual. I exhale my frustration.

'You know the drill. I'll check in on you two later.' He turns to the girl

'Noble will look after you.' He smiles at her before turning to the door.

'No!' I raise my voice. 'I'm not having another Spare. Isn't there someone else who can teach her?' Stevens comes up to me, his happy demeanour gone. He puts his face level with mine. His large frame would normally put fear into anyone. I'm not afraid but I do feel intimidated. I try my best to stand firm.

'You know it's not up to me. I'd put her with someone better than *you* if it was my choice.' He says in a gruff whisper that only I can hear. We've not always seen eye-to-eye. He straightened up turning his back on us both before exiting out the door he came through. I run my hands through my hair as I exhale again before turning to her. She's shaking, her eyes wide. She's terrified. Once again, my heart goes out to her. She's obviously had a bad time.

My annoyance ebbed, knowing that despite how I feel, neither of us had a choice. Spare had to go where help was needed.

'Are you ok?' I ask her genuinely. Her mouth moves likes she's trying to answer. 'What? Not use to someone asking how you are?' I joke.

'n-no. N-not really.' She manages and pauses before continuing. 'I-I don't remember the last time someone asked me that...without the answer having to be 'yeah I'm fine, and you?'

Ah, social interaction acknowledgement. Saying 'how are you' when actually meaning hello. Goodness this poor girl. Silence. Meeting new people is always awkward.

'I'm Jake, by the way. Jacob actually but I prefer Jake.'

'Lina.' She's has a look of a creature in Craft lights. She's still shaking.

'When did you last eat?' I ask her. Lack of food can cause shaking. I can tell something's happened to her but being low on blood sugar isn't going to help.

I see her eyes dart from side to side for a few seconds before she shakes her head to say 'I don't know'.

'Come with me.' I tell her and walk round to the kitchen area. I look through the cupboards trying to find something but they're mostly empty so I make something out of it with the aim that it's something slightly edible. The best I could come up with was some porridge with fruit. Not a lot but it's all that was there. Looks like Arden has been raiding the cupboards again. She certainly has an appetite. I leave her in peace for about 10 mins while I raided my tool box for spare wires for the craft. She finds me once she's finished but remains quiet until I realise she's there.

'Ok now?' I check.

'Bit better.' She replies. Not knowing what to say to her we stay there in painful silence.

We can't stay here in awkward silence. I look at her suitcase.

'I'll show you to the room.' I offer and tell her simultaneously heading towards the door. 'Do you want me to take that for you?' I indicate her suitcase but she shakes her head.

We go up 2 floors to the accommodation floor in more silence. I can't think of anything to say. I didn't want an apprentice, they knew that, yet, here I am. Leo would've got it.

I scan my card to unlock door 293 and into our room.

He held the door open for me. I look around. Another kitchen area with a small fridge, kettle and a container of tea. Jake flicks the switch on the kettle. The side of the room that has the window has 2 wardrobes, 2 chest of drawers and a full length mirror.

'This is your bed' Jake indicates to the bed nearest the bathroom door. My gaze falls on it. It looks un-comfy and worn with a cold black metal frame. Nothing like home. My eyes wonder to the floor, cold, hard concrete. No carpet, no laminate flooring. I look to the other side of the room. Another frame, another worn mattress. Two beds!

'We share a room?' I asked shocked.

'Yep.' Her answers bluntly sitting on his bed. 'Spare and apprentice share regardless of gender. Says in the handbook… didn't you know?' no I certainly didn't know. I can't take it all in. It's so different here. Nothing like home. My breath gets stuck in my throat and I can't breathe. Hot tears fill my eyes and I fall to the floor, burying my face in my hands.

Crap she's crying! What do I do? Why is she crying? I drop of the bed to the floor beside. I hesitate. What am I meant to do? I can't hug her, I've only just met her. It'd be weird. I decide putting my hand on her shoulder is best.

'Hey, I know this isn't exactly a castle but it's what we've got.' I'm awful at this. The kettle switch flips off letting me know the water is boiling. *'That's it!'* I think as I place my hands on her upper arms, gently making her stand and sit on what was now her bed. I then get up and make 2 cups of tea, leaving her to cry for a bit.

'Here.' I say to her a short while later. She's calmed down a bit. I hold the steaming mug out to her when she lifts her head.

'Thank you' she manages a small smile as she takes the mug. A warm feeling fills my chest as I look at this fragile young woman. I sit down beside her.

'My mum always said 'nothing can't be fixed with a good cup of tea.' She smiles, almost laughs. She has a nice smile.

'Believed?' she asked noticing the past tense.

'She died when I was 18. It was always just me and her.' I say gruffly, upset by the thought.

'Sorry.' She says.

'Don't be.' I turn to her. 'She was sick for a while.'

'What was her name?'

'Seren.'

'Pretty. What did she die of?' she sounds cautious, like she is carefully choosing her words. She needn't worry about hurting me. The thought alone does that. I miss her.

'Cancer.' I say. She apologises again. People say that when they don't know what to say, but she sounds genuine. I watch her as she drinks. What could've made this girl so sad? Would it be rude to ask? I've never been one to hold back.

'So what happened?' I ask bluntly. No point beating around the bush. She looks at me, surprised by my forwardness.

'Look,' I continue, 'if I'm to train you then we're going to be spending a lot of time together. We might as well be friends during it.'

I feel dumbfounded. If it wasn't for the fact I have to track this guy I'd say he was sweet in a rough round the edges kind of way. I'm trying to be kind, taking an interest in his mum. I need him to trust me. I'm a mess. What am I meant to say? I'm here for a reason. Aren't people with an agenda meant to be suave and charming? Yet, here's me, falling like a t-rex, being crushed by my own weight and struggling to get myself together. He's tried to be kind to me. Making tea. He's a little direct but he's sweet in a way. I was rather taken aback when he asked me what had happened. I hadn't even thought about him asking. I have the story of being made redundant, but why should I lie? I oddly feel like I should tell him the truth. He has those eyes, crystal blue, trusting but had been hurt before. I can't tell him the truth though. I don't think I can do this. But I must...

'A family member is missing.' Not a lie but not the truth either. 'Everything is wrong right now. I'm not at home. This isn't my room and this isn't my bed. My whole world has changed in less than a day and it's a lot to take in.' I tear up again, letting out a shaky breath to calm myself. 'Nothing feels right at the moment. I can't help find her and I feel useless as well as out of sorts. Everything I knew is gone.'

'Tough day then.' Is all he can say. I laugh at his understatement.

'Something like that.' I agree, tears falling for the hundredth time today. I look at him. His blue eyes looking at me. His strong jaw set firm. He looks sad.

'I hope they find her.' He says quietly.

'Same.'

It's odd. This stranger sat beside me. This guy who I know has a past. He is the only one who has made me feel calm. Just by listening. He hasn't said much, hardly anything to be honest, but he's listened. My world is coming down around me...and I feel a lot calmer than I did this morning.

I drain my cup and get up. 'Stay here for a bit if you need to. I've got to get that blasted craft flying by tonight so if you need me I'll be there.' I say as I put my cup on the side. It's a bit of an excuse. Something about her makes me feel different. I don't know how but I need to have some time alone. It's probably just sympathy. She seems a nice girl having a hard time. Poor thing must be going through her own personal hell. I feel for her, I really do. Someone close to you suddenly gone and you can't do anything to help or bring them back. It's definitely a feeling I wouldn't wish on anybody. A raw feeling that never really eases.

I don't usually tell people that much about me when I first meet them but it just seemed to slip out. It felt nice to tell her. Why though? I've only just met her.

I make my way back to the garage, leaving her alone, and climb up onto the craft. I wish this wires would fit and work. I usually can work out the problem...yet I keep thinking of her.

Trust

That night I was restless. I couldn't sleep. The bed wasn't comfortable. The room was strange. The pillow was flat. After hours of tossing and turning unable to get to sleep. My mind filled with memories of Lyra. My precious girl. I remember her being put into my arms for the first time. A tiny humanoid that had made me look so big. Her tiny hands, her equally tiny feet. I cried then too, but in amazement.

Sitting with the duvet cocooned around me for comfort I immersed myself in my memories. Her first smile, her first coo, babbling away in noises like she was trying to talk to me. The first time I heard her laugh is still my favourite sound ever. Her tiny body crawling across my bedroom floor and her first steps across her room played out like a film. I welled up with happiness and pride all over again as though it was the first time. The memory of her just made the hole in my chest feel vastly bigger aching like a ton in weight was upon me.

The thought of her being hurt ruminates my mind again and anger boils in the pit of my stomach. A blackness grows churning and knotting in pure hate. If she is hurt in anyway when she is found, I will hunt them down and kill them myself.

I hold onto this darkness for a while. I wallow, allowing it to take over. It makes me feel like I have some form of control.

Slowly a dim light catches the corner of my eye. The Bio Orb has been shaken.

'You still awake? Its 3am.' Jake tells me checking the time. 3am? Damn. I didn't even know it was that late. I hear the mattress creak as he sits up. 'Are you alright?' I shake my head. I want to sleep I'm so tired but I'm too wide awake. 'You know we have to be up in a few hours, right?' I nod. 'Do you want to talk about it?' I do but it will give me away if I do. I shake my head again, the extent of my nonverbal communication. 'Is there anything I can do?' he asks. I feel guilty. He's been so nice to me so far and right now, more than ever, I need a friend but I have to keep him at arm's length.

I shake my head once more. 'No, it's ok. Go back to sleep.'

'Look...I get that losing someone close to you is hard. Trust me, I get it but you're not going to be any good to anyone if you don't keep looking after yourself.' I hate that he's so nice. It'd be so much easier if he wasn't. 'We need to be up soon. Try to get some sleep.' He lies back down, light still glowing dimly. I lie down too. I doubt I'll be able to sleep though.

The alarm wakes me up at 7. I never hit snooze so I'm out of bed straight away. I run my rough hands over my face to get rid of the sleepiness. Sitting on my bed I look at Lina. Fast asleep with the pillow half over her head and her hair in her face. I almost laugh but despite the funny sleeping position, she looks peaceful. I hate to wake her but I have to. I make fresh tea and place one beside her. I don't even know if I made it right. She never complained yesterday so I made it with milk and 1 sugar. I gently shake her shoulder only to be met with the pillow in my face.

'Go away.' She moans.

'Sorry, but I live here.' She almost jumps out of her skin like she suddenly remembers where she is. 'Didn't mean to scare you. We need to be in the garage by 8. I'm going to have a shower.'

Letting the hot water pour down me I take longer than usual. Partly to give her some time and privacy. Partly because everything feels a lot more *there* today. I'm suddenly self-aware. I'm aware of the glass around me and the distance between it and myself. I'm aware of my body and how every sense in me is on edge. I'm aware of her being the other side if the wall. What is this? It wasn't like this when I woke up yesterday. It's got to be her. I'm not use to having to coach a female Spare. That's got to be it. It just different and new. Nothing more.

I step out of the shower, wrap my towel around my waist and take a look round. I left my clothes in the room. *Can't I just stay here?* I ask myself with my head against the door. This sudden awareness is throwing me. I don't feel like me. I can't stay here forever though.

Slowly I open the door and peer in. she's up. That's a start. She's looking at herself in the mirror, hand on stomach and she goes from side to side in just her dark blue jeans and white bra. I lose the air in my lungs. Why does she have to be pretty? I can't stay hiding in this bathroom. I need to be at the garage or Stevens will be on my case again. Taking a breath to steady my nerve I walk in.

'You look fine, woman.' I try to joke. She whirls around startled grabbing her pillow to cover herself.

'What do you think you're doing?' she asks, stressed that I caught her indecent. Eyes still wide she looks me up and down. 'You're naked.' The fact dawning on her. She turn around as if it will make it less award.

'Well that is usually the norm when showering.' I reply suddenly even more aware of my bare chest. Silence. I see my clothes on my chest of drawers on the other side of the room. Think Jake. It's can't get any more awkward. 'Uh-bathroom's free.' I offer as an icebreaker as cold drops of water fall from my slicked back hair and down my arms.

'Thanks' she says not looking me in the eye as she turns and beelines for the bathroom. I step aside to let her by, knocking her tea that she'd placed on the side by the kettle over and spilling it all over the clothes she'd laid out the previous night. I apologise doing the only thing I can think to do and that is grab one of my shirts for her. I apologise again as she gingerly takes my shirt still hugging the pillow to her. A moment of silence passes again, I'm still in just a towel as the door closes and I feel relief and embarrassment rush through me.

'You bloody idiot Jake.' I say to myself before rushing to get dressed and leave like a little boy who doesn't want to get in trouble.

I find Jake at the garage talking to a Fleet Pilot about, judging from the direction of the arm gestures, the air craft that's just been brought in. This morning was embarrassing. Anyone would've thought I'd never seen a semi naked guy before. I panicked when he came spoke first. I hadn't even heard him come into the room. I was looking at my stretch marks in the mirror, remembering that my baby was once in there. Safe. He might have seen them. I'm scared he'll ask about them. If

40

it does then I'll have to admit about being a mother and that could lead into me telling him about tracking him because he's the only link to our lead. I wasn't expecting him to be in just his towel. I don't know why. What was I expecting? Him to come out of a shower fully clothed in his best suit? Stupid me. I let my guard down. I tried not to look at his body but I couldn't help catching a glance, especially as he was in nothing but a towel. I liked what I saw but I can't think of that. I have more important things to think about than ogling a toned torso. Not overly tone, not defined 6 pack to speak of but enough to know he was in shape. He also has a tattoo on his upper arm. A planet with a ring of small stars around it. I like it- get it together Lina!

I walk in, head down, allowing as much of my mid brown hair, from my low ponytail, to fall in my face as possible. His shirt covers my hands. Dark blue sleeves with a white body is comfortably baggy. My Cariopius hidden in my boot.

I lean against the adjacent kitchen side. Jake finishes up with the pilot and clocks me there. He makes his way over and my stomach goes into knots.

'Ok?' he asks and I nod. 'This guy needs an engine check. We better get started.'

Quick and to the point. A regular thing with him. Straight to the point. I follow him to the hydraulic jack in which the craft rests. Taking a power tool he removes the streamlined panel to reveal the engine. Quickly he loosens the engine so it can be removed. High tech which can withstand high speeds and enemy fire but can be removed so easily. He proceeds by taking a hoist and attaching the engine before removing it completely from the craft.

'Where did you learn to do that? That was so quick.' I say impressed by the swiftness of the well-practised motion.

'Been doing it all my life really. Use to take my toys apart to see how it all worked.' He tells me. 'Slowly went from toys to my hover boards.'

'You had a hover board?' I ask childlike excitement in my voice. 'I always wanted one of those.'

'How come you didn't?' he asks

'Dad said it was 'too dangerous'' I reply recalling the disappointment. 'So it took dedication to manage to put everything back together again?' I ask half mocking.

'Use to send my mum mad with all the mess.' He smiles before remembering his mum and the smile fades and he turns to the tools behind me. It must still be a raw memory.

I feel sorry for him, all on his own. Lyra she's on her own. Focus!

'What do we need to do?' I decided it was safer to focus on the task at hand rather than prompt him to talk more about his past. I still need to build trust.

'Just take it apart cover it in this. It's almost out. It's why it's not working properly.' He hands me a jar of a thick, almost clear paste. There's no smell and it leaves my hand greasy.

'What is it?' I ask dumbfounded by this strange jar I couldn't think what on Lucinesri it was meant to be.

'Backaka oil.'

'For real? I use this in my hair?' backaka oil. The oil from a backaka tree. Discovered when humans first came to Lucinesri. They found the oil can be used for multiple things such as conditioner and a skin moisturiser, you can even eat it. I didn't know it was used for mechanics. 'Why is it used in mechanics?'

'It has multiple uses, beauty and health stuff mainly but a lot of people don't realise that it can be used for crafts. It keeps the cylinders and valves lubricated enough to keep it running for months at a time. Also it's a preferred method because-thanks to King Vulcan- we don't have to dig deep into the ground and use the natural resources from under the crust.'

'I'm impressed.' I admit to him ignoring his sarcastic tone at the mention of my grandfather. Anyone who knows me would know I wouldn't admit that easily. He looks at me like I'm joking. 'I didn't know that.'

'You're impressed by that?' he sounds like he doesn't believe me.

'Well...yeah. It's resourceful, shows you know what you're on about. I'm amazed by how it all works! Every piece going together to works simultaneously to make it fly... Shows dedication...' I trail off. A bit embarrassed by my enthusiasm while explaining why I'm impressed. I like that he knows about the tools he works with. I like that he's aware of the uses and planetary resources that is used to.

Wasn't expecting her to be impressed by the use of backaka oil. It's what I use every day. It's just an everyday thing. She also said she was impressed by what I knew. I guess it does take dedication to know all this that I'm teaching her. It oddly made me feel...appreciated. It was odd...in a good way. When she isn't looking I feel...happy. Silently thank her. It feels good. The next few days pass without problem. Lina is picking it up fast. I quite like her company. I feel a bit guilty for trying to dismiss her so quickly. She's smart but doesn't like waking up in the mornings. She'll get use to the routine I'm sure.

I tell her about the cock pit made from aluminium, fan hub, compressors and fuselage connectors to the retractable wings. Cock pits made from carbon fibre beneath a complex motherboard of wires and connectors linking the buttons to its individual chain of events to an action.

After a couple of days I told her about Leo. A Spare that was assigned to me a few years after I became a Fleet Mechanic. I didn't think to go over the dangers of mixing the wires and there was an explosion. He got facial burns and lost his leg and couldn't work with us anymore. He's fine though, he's now married with a child. The incident gave me trust issues about myself though.

I didn't want another Spare after that but I like Lina being around.

The next few days past like this, each one feeling like a lifetime. How long do I have to wait until I start prying information out of him? I feel like my energy is draining away and getting up each morning is like climbing a mountain. I still can't sleep very well. I wake up in the night and Jake's gone. I don't know where he goes. The first time I found him gone I panicked that he'd somehow figured it out and ran away. He was there in the morning though. I like Jake's company, he can make light of a situation. Even make me smile. I wish it wasn't like this. I feel tired all the time and I don't have as much enthusiasm as normal. The only thing getting me through it is the thought of seeing my daughter again.

Jake has a lease on life I wish I did. He jumps from the heights of the hydraulic lifts, seemingly, without a second thought. He's skilled in all the tools using them with ease whereas I'm more 'slow and steady'. He has so much confidence and skill and, at times, I can't even get a word out without tripping over that.

Luckily, he's patient too. He helps me when I can't stop shaking, just talks to me. He remains calm when I mess up the welding and get myself into an emotional mess over it. One thing I feel over and over again is how calm I feel being next to him.

After a week of gaining trust, me and Jake are talking about whether or not we believe in Scarisys, a mythical creature with sharp teeth and strong wings with razor sharp claws, silent and elusive that no one is sure actually exists. I believe that they could exist whereas Jake is sceptical. We are getting deep into conversation when the door opens. We both look up. My stomach falls and I feel immediately guilty again when Colonel Stevens and Commander Costello walk in. what on Lucinesri is he doing here? Does he have news?

'Here we have one of our mechanic units.' Stevens motions to the garage before turning his attention to us. 'He we have Mr Noble and new Spare, Miss Mond. Commander Costello is doing an inspection of all the Fleet units.' He informs us.

'Would it be convenient if I could have a word with miss...?' I'm unsure is he actually has forgotten the alias name that was literally just mentioned or if he's trying to make it look as though we don't know each other.

'Mond.' I pipe up quickly and stepping forward so we can talk. We slowly meander to the far side of the garage where we can't be heard. He asks me questions like 'how are you finding your new line of work?' to keep up the illusion until he's sure we're out of ear shot.

'What do you know?' he asks quietly in his gruff voice.

'Not much yet,' I answer honestly, 'but I think I've established trust.'

'Good.' Costello says. 'Now try and get something out of him. You've had a week.'

K.Phelps

'I believe it was you who said it'd take more than 'a few days' was it not?' I retort not appreciating the insinuation that I was doing nothing before I calm my tone. 'Do you know anything?'

'Some reported sightings but nothing definite and so far all our leads have drawn blanks.' He tells me, sounding ashamed. 'There's a possibility we've missed something so we're going back over all the evidence.'

'So I've got further than you?' I'm hurt and annoyed. 'I'm here, everything I know gone and *you* have to go back over it all because you might have missed something? Are you for real?'

'It's just a precaution.' He tries to reason but we both know that it's lies. 'Keep doing what you're doing. Stay close and get what you can out of this...' he looks at Jake and seethes. 'Scum, lowlife criminal...'

'Don't you dare!' I order unexpectedly raising my voice slightly. Luckily not enough to draw attention. Now Costello was seething at me. 'You don't know him. He's a young man who had a troubled past and made some mistakes. If you're going to belittle someone based on mistakes. If you're going to be cruel, at least aim at something they can help.'

'Oh yeah, like what?' he sneers, obviously angry that I've gone against him. That's the problem with me and Costello. He's a big, intimidating figure that's high in the Fleet and I'm short and unassuming. In the Fleet he's above me in the hierarchy and outside of the Fleet I'm a princess and above him. The conflicting roles between us often leads us to butt heads.

'Like you being an arsehole.' I fire back. He growls at me, making sure we aren't being watched he speaks to me in a tone I've never heard him use before.

'I'd be careful, Princess. Don't go getting to close. You might be disappointed.' He warned before straightening up.

'Right! Thank you Miss Mond. That'll be all.' He says loud enough to get the attention of Jake and Stevens. He stays for a while, to play on the inspection excuse, before leaving and I can breathe again. I am thankful he is helping to look for Lyra. He's one of the best in the Fleet. I'm not sorry though. He didn't need to speak about Jake that way.

I look out the window to see it was getting dark out. I need some air so I silently leave the room. I'm not sure where I'm going but I'll find somewhere.

I found her on the roof leaning against the railing, looking up at the night sky. I joined her against the railing, looking up, trying to see what she could see. Both moons, Aku, a large silver-blue planet and Jaci, a smaller planet, pink in hue are both visible from this position. Clusters of distant stars giving a milking appearance in the sky above in multiple colours. Below the city of Vulcadon lay beneath us. One side of the city, mountains bordering around the forest and on the other side a beech of ice blue that contain a kind of bio luminescence and glowed in the dark. Not far from the shore was an island.

'Do you ever wonder what's out there?' she asked without breaking her gaze with the galaxy.

'What? Besides the planets and lives everyone escaped from?'

'Yeah, I mean...think about it. What if there are Beings we haven't encountered yet? What if there's lifestyles that could give us a better way of living for us and this planet that we haven't even considered?' she explained, passion growing in her voice as she spoke, only now, I couldn't take my eyes off of her. This amazing girl, seeing the galaxy differently to everyone. We have restriction bought on by fear from our homes and she sees opportunity to unite and expand ourselves.

Happiness, just from looking at her, rising in my chest. How is she able to see everything with such an open mind?

Slowly, her expression turned from one of wonder to one of concern.

'Do...do you think...our families are out there? I never knew my mum, maybe she's out there...and you dad-'

'He's not my dad. A dad stays around even if he isn't with your mum.' Any mention of him makes me instantly withdraw. I don't want to talk or even think about him ever again.

'Sorry...'

'Don't be. I shouldn't have said anything.' She knows he isn't about. She doesn't know the whole story but her question was innocent. She goes to walk away

'I do by the way.' Looking at her. 'I do think he's out there. Where, on the other hand, is something I'd rather not know.'

'I keep thinking about her' I know she's on about her missing family member. She never says a name or how they're related. 'I keep feeling guilty.'

'Why?'

'I keep thinking I should've been able to help her. If she can go missing in a place that is supposed to be safe then...then everything I know is wrong. I don't know what to believe anymore.'

I don't know what happened with this family member but I know it wasn't her fault.

'And then there's you.' She continues.

'Me?' I ask confused

'When I'm with you I can, just for a moment, forget it all but then I catch myself and I feel guilty all over again. I just want her back.'

I can't even comprehend how she must be feeling. How does she not explode? Surely feeling all that is a bad thing. I pull her into a hug. She needs it and I want to hold her. She resists at first but gives in wrapping her arms around my waist and my heart skips. Her head fits perfectly on my shoulder and I rest my head on hers. I could hold her forever. Her air smells sweet. She shivers and we break apart. Without thinking I take off my jacket and drape it over her shoulders. Her eyes are wet again. I wish I could make her happy or even just distracts her...

I've got it!

'Come with me' I tell her taking her by the hand. 'There's something I want you to see.' I lead her to a disused garage in the building.

I take her to the deepest part of the building. Very few Beings know that there are 3 disused floors beneath ground level. You can only get to it by stairs providing you know where they are. It's cooler down here and she puts her arms in my jacket to keep her warm. Its pitch black as I run my hands over the door trying to find the handle. It's the same as I blindly make my way through the room for a certain switch. I pull it when I find it and the generator comes to life filling the room with light. It's dim at first but everything comes into view as it gets brighter.

I didn't know there were underground floors here. I'm blown away as the light gets brighter and everything comes into view as my eyes adjust to the light again. On one side of the room lies a makeshift table with blue prints. Not far from that are beaten up tool boxes presumably kept from being scrapped and filled with a multitude of equipment. A few books scattered here and there and right in the centre of the room is a craft. Is this where he's been going at night? An aircraft sat before me. Different to a usual aircraft. It was smooth in shape, more streamlined. Its bare metal shone in the light. Even its booster jets were more streamlined. Wires and gizmos hung out from part of the jet like spaghetti.

'What is this?' I ask amazed

'I've been building it.' he says

'you *built* this?!' is he serious?! He actually built this? How? Where would you even begin? It's amazing.

'Yeah. When I need to get stress out I come down here and work. It's not finished yet.' He tells me walking up to the spaghetti wires. 'I want to make this the fastest aircraft in the world. Maybe get it used in the Fleet. Maybe I'll get recognition finally.' He has the look of someone who's been knocked back no matter how hard he tries.

'How are you going to make it the fastest?' I ask. Like a flash he grabs the blueprints from the table and lays them out in front of us on the ground by the wires.

He's so enthusiastic and passionate when explaining his idea to me I can't help but admire the glow coming from him as he speaks about the aerodynamics of the design and how he wants to hide mini turbines into the exterior connected to an energy saving generator. He tells me he hopes it'll be more energy efficient as well as more reliant.

'Have you got it to fly yet?' she asks sounding interested.

'Sort of.' I admit, embarrassed. 'I managed to get it a few feet off the ground but it's too heavy to go any further. I've reduced the size of the generator but still hasn't worked.' She looks thoughtful for a moment mulling over my words.

'What's the exterior made of?'

'Steel. Why?'

'Aluminium. It's lighter.' She pauses, thinking. 'Let's see the fans.' I hand them to her and she inspects them by rotating them in her hand and spinning the propellers. 'Is there any way you can change the angle on these propellers slightly?' she asks. 'You might get more spin speed and make them more powerful.'

My mind goes blank and I just stare at her in amazement.

'I did well in science.' She admits shyly. This girl has done nothing but amaze me since I met her. How can a person so perfect exist? Also, where can I get aluminium from?

Why do I get self-conscious when I talk about what I know? My embarrassment turns to selfishness as my thoughts turn to Lyra. If we could get this thing flying, I could find her.

'I'd be happy to help, you know, if you would like me to.' I offer with selfish intentions. He half smiles and my heart races before snapping back into grief. To be honest I'm exhausted, mentally and physically from going back and forth between a moment of peace and crippling grief. I don't believe I can handle it much longer.

He hands me a screwdriver and guides me on what to do. We work late into the night until the only thing left to do is get some aluminium to create a new frame.

We rest beside each other, tired and my head resting on his shoulder. My heart feel like a heavy weight is tied to it. I feel so selfish. I have to use this guy's kindness in the hopes of manipulating him to lead me to my daughter. I don't want to hurt him but I want my daughter more. Either way I'm going to end up hurt but so is one of them if I don't. I want Lyra back desperately but I can't stand to hurt him.

The sweet smell of her hair fill my lungs again. My stomach flips. She works well and has been a big help. I don't know what I'd do without her now. Tomorrow is going to be hard with a few hours' sleep. I don't care. This has been worth it.

We sit in contented silence for a bit, my eyes heavy and my heart conflicted but I still allow myself to enjoy the company. I adjust myself so I face him more, hugging his arm. I feel myself starting to drift of but I'm woken as Jake adjusts himself to look at me. His blue eyes locking with mine. He brushes some lose hair away from my face. My heart racing, pounding against my chest.

I look into her eyes. Is it premature to see a future with her? It's not been that long. Just looking at her leave me breathless. Sweeping her hair from her face lets me see her better. She's everything. She's not breaking eye contact. I decide to take the risk. I lean in.

He kisses me. Soft and sweet. I kiss back wanting nothing but him. His arms wrap around my waist and I pull him closer. To feel something different is a relief. This could easily lead to more. I want more. A niggling thought enters my head and won't go away. It can't concentrate. The reason I'm here. Lyra. I pull away quickly no longer filled with relief or with his arms making me feel safe but now with panic. What am I doing? Am I that stupid? I can't be doing this. I can't breath and my chest feels tight. I need out. He's apologising. What for? I run and he calls after me.

'Lina? Lina!' I ignore him just running for the first place I can think of.

Did I do something wrong? Does she not feel the same? Maybe I'm seeing something that isn't there? I run after her but it's so dark on these levels that when I get to the ground floor she's gone. Where is she?

I woke up with a fright the next morning as the door banged open. I rubbed the sleep from my eyes as the room came into vision. Hydraulic jacks, an air craft from yesterday. I slept in the garage. My shoulder goes cold as I sit up and see that I used Jake's jacket as a blanket. I pull it back on and stretch. My head feels light but I feel physically sick. Glancing up I see Jake standing there. He looks tired and hurt. It's enough for pain to tear through my chest.

Rigidly I get up and walk towards the door. I stop as go to pass him. A lump forms in my throat.

'I'm sorry.' I tell him trying not to let tears fall. 'It's not what you think I swear...it's complicated.'

'How is it not what I think?' I wasn't expecting him to talk to me so his question caught me off-guard. 'I looked for you last night. After you ran off. I thought you felt something for me.' I can feel the truth threatening to spill out. I can't tell him the truth. Panic soars through me and I hastily turn and make my exit, forcing myself not to look back.

I speed walk to our room without stopping and only taking a breath once the bathroom door is locked behind me. I strip off and allow the hot water fall down on me. Of course I have feelings for him. I allow myself to cry. Angry, hard sobs. What is wrong with me? I need to do this to find Lyra. The thought-which is becoming a real possibility- of never seeing her again feels like having my heart torn out. the pain in my chest the feel of falling in the pit of my stomach which also feels like I'm going to throw up, the breath escaping my lungs and I feel like I'm being strangled. I can hardly talk, I break out on a cold sweat just from the thought. How did I get myself into this? Jake makes me feel safe, like something I can feel control with. Sanity. He makes me laugh, he makes me smile and just for a moment, one teeny tiny split second I can forget and feel peace. Am I just displacing my emotions? Am I attaching myself to him in my need for support and security? Is it because I need someone to hold me and comfort me? What if when I get her back and my feelings disappear? Curled up on the floor of the shower I feel like I need him right now. I need someone. I can't do this anymore.

Jake

She had the look of fear I seen the day I met her. I thought she felt the same. Of course she doesn't. Why would she? No one has every cared for me. Except 2 people. How could I possibly think she'd be interested in a low life like me? Stevens thinks I'm worthless. The Fleet wrote me off because I wouldn't go against family. My own father didn't think I was worth it.

Growing up wasn't bad I guess. My mum worked in the city's farm fields where the whole city gets their food from. Large open fields full of crops. It was decided many years ago that if you work you get food. There are exceptions of course, like if you're ill. She always came home worn out and tired but she always made an effort for me.

I remember her saying goodbye to me in the mornings after dropping me off at nursery. A friend of hers would take me home with arms full of pictures of colourful scribbles I drew and said each one was an aircraft and boxes glued together to make, what was supposed to be, an aircraft also although it probably looked more like a sorry mess of tissue paper windows and misshapen cardboard wings cut by the hand of a small boy inexperienced with scissors.

I would take each one home and wait patiently, eagerly staring up at the clock even though I couldn't tell the time then. I would sit with my teddy bear opposite me, pretending he was a giant who needed to be taken down by the Fleet. I would zoom around the room with my miniature replicas trying to take down the giant.

In my head I was the pilot of the craft, making the sound effect with my mouth.

'Zooooooom! Zap! Zap! Zap! Pew! Pew! Take that evil giant!' I'd yell at the inanimate stuffed creature.

I'd run to the door as fast I my legs would carry me as soon as I heard the door open shouting for my mum. She'd have dark circles under her eyes and would be resting against the wall exhausted from her day of harvesting the crops. As soon as she'd see me her would always put on a brave face and smile brightly at me scooping me up in her arms and hugging me tightly. I'd practically drag her by her hand into the room where I was playing to proudly show her my work that I'd done that day. She was always impressed by my efforts, even if it was just to humour or encourage me either way it made me feel proud of myself. She probably got sick of pretending to be surprised by my multiple scribble drawings and hap hazard models.

She'd talk to me about what I'd done that day, if I'd had a good day as she sits me to the table with my toys while she made dinner. Sometimes she'd give me a butter knife and a spare vegetable to 'cut' up for her. She'd always cook it as well, making sure I had what I'd 'cooked myself'. She always highlighted what I'd done well and whatever I didn't do so well she'd advise me how I could do better next time and encouraged me to try again.

I'd show my father the same excitement as he came through the door too. I'd run up shouting his name and begging him to come look at my drawings but he'd hardly look at me. Instead, he'd lightly ruffle my hair and say, 'maybe later' and walk by to the kitchen for his food. Of course, little me would be upset. I'd sit in the living room with my drawings and wait for him to come and sit down. Unfortunately he would go up to their room, leaving my work unseen and unappreciated. I remember how disappointed I felt. It seems stupid now but 3 year old me would be heart broken. I'd always see it as 'dad will see it and he'll be happy and proud at how much of a big boy I am' but it never happened. He would always come in, have dinner and leaves us so he could retreat upstairs and pretend that we didn't exist. At least that's how it felt.

On the rare occasion that he would sit with us, I'd always try and get him to play with me, do the puzzle or play craft races with me...but he never did. He'd sit there using grunts to respond or he would get up and go to the garage to 'fix' whatever was broken. I'd follow him desperate for his attention.

As I got older I would still go to the garage where he was. This time it was to take my hover board or some other machinery apart and either putting them back together or enhancing them. I hope my father would come and take an interest. Show me how to use the tools or work with me but it was like I was invisible. I tried so hard and it was all pointless. My mum tried to talk to him but he wasn't interested. He ignored her too. Wouldn't kiss her goodbye, say thank you to her or ask her how she was. It was like a complete stranger living in our home. Only this was the person who was meant to look after us.

I looked like him. Same hair colour, same build and same facial features. I have my mother's eye colour though... and her kindness. I don't know how I would be, in fact I hate to think how I would be if it wasn't for her love and care. Unfortunately I still wanted love and care from my presently absent father. Although he was there he never looked after us.

Just before I turned 8 I would hear my parents arguing after I'd gone to bed. I'd stay awake hearing them. I might not have really been old enough to understand but I knew things weren't great between them. My father would start an argument over small things like not putting the dishes away when that was my chore. It would continue the rest of the night. Bickering and snide remarks from him anytime he spoke. The atmosphere was almost unbearable. I'd often stay in my room but I would stay with my mum so she didn't have to be with him alone. I tried to stand up for her and tell him to leave her alone but as normal it fell on deaf ears. The invisible boy not seen again.

One night my father's voice was a lot louder than usual, I could quite make out what he was shouting about but I couldn't make a word out. I could hear my mum trying to keep her voice down, her words were strained. I pulled the duvet around me tighter. I hated the fighting. Why was he like that? I always thought I must've done something for him to hate us so much. Was it my fault?

My 8ᵗʰ birthday came and went. As usual my mum made a fuss. A present, a cake and something fun to do even if it was just a trip to the park to run around and get all my energy out. She always tried to make me happy. I wish I had appreciated her more at that time.

Not long after another fight broke out, this time I heard things, cups probably smash and shatter. I bolted out of bed and to the top of the stairs. I listened.

He was shouting and she was crying. It sounded like she was begging, saying 'please, please don't.' don't what? He only replied in anger. He said he couldn't pretend anymore. He couldn't do this anymore. He never wanted this. Doors slammed and voices grew louder. They got to the stairs and he heavy feet stomped up.

'What are you doing up?!' he shouted as he saw me huddled on the top step. He stomped past me and forced their bedroom door open so hard he banged against the wall. My mum stayed by me, her arms around me as I watched him grab a bag and pack his stuff into it. Fear prickled my body as it dawned on me what was happening. I ran from my mum and to his side. I grabbed the bag shouting for him not to go but he pushed me away. I landed on the floor. He ignored me again and carried on packing. My mum rushed to my side and I held her tight. Why was he leaving?

Not another word was said until the front door slammed shut and we both broke down crying. It hurt so much. He wasn't exactly a role model or even active in my life but him leaving felt like losing a part of me. My chest hurt ached in a pain I'd never experienced before and it felt like my small 8 year old body would explode. Mum and

I held each other for what felt like forever. We cried until we cried ourselves out. She promised me that it was to do with them and that she didn't want me to feel like it was my fault.

We didn't sleep that night. The next few days and weeks were odd. His absence was felt. Mum cried for nights on end. She tried to make out it was fine and tried to carry on as normal but I could see she was upset. It hurt her as much as it did me. She always looked like she'd been crying. She tried to be happy at my pictures but it felt different, like it was forced.

I figured he never wanted a family. He never wanted me. I don't know what he was 'pretending' to do because he never acted like a dad.

As I got to my teens I had become an angry person. I shouted at everyone. I played up in school. I'd talk back, wouldn't do the work in class. I would skip class too.

Rebelling soon went from playing up at school to getting in with the wrong crowd. I started shoplifting. Just small things but it quickly became bigger things. My mum said it was because of my friends and how they were influencing me but I still felt like the decision was mine. Eventually I would go off on my own and find cordoned off places and hover board there, testing out the modifications. I would zoom across the plantations, ignoring the world. Feeling the wind rush past me and the flip in my stomach from the thrill. It made me feel free. At least it did until security or the authorities showed up.

The look of disappointment on my mother's face when they would bring me home will stay with me forever. I remember them holding my roughly by the arms and banging on our front door. My mum answered, her friend was visiting, the smile quickly wiped off her face and her colour drained when she saw me with authorities in tow. I'd been charged with trespassing (just like I had a few times before as well as with petty theft) and they destroyed my hover board. They said that if I was caught again for the same offences I would be sent to a Secure Training Centre. I really didn't care what happened to me by that point. I didn't see me having any kind of future.

Of course, mum went off on one, yelling at me desperately trying to make me see sense and not to waste all the potential I didn't believe I had. She was already stressed enough with work and keeping our home together without me being in trouble with the law.

I always felt worthless and that she'd have an easier life without me. So I did the same thing as my father, I packed a bag and left. I didn't have a plan but I felt that if I left she'd have one less worry.

I made my way through the streets in the dark. The only light came from the street lights filled with Bio Orbs. I passed houses seeing families together.

Eventually I came across an abandoned house on the edge of the city and decided to stay there the night. Good thing to as it started to rain. I stayed in the doorway watching the rain fall. I listened as it patted on the road. I was sat there a while when a weathered voice spoke snapping me out of my trance and making me jump.

'What're you doing 'ere?' the voice said. 'Shouldn't ya be at home, boy?' I just stared into the darkness of the room. Where had the voice come from? I felt scared and I stayed put suddenly feeling like my shoes had weights in them.

'Well don't just sit there, get ye self in out thik doorway.' He ordered. I don't think I ever moved so quickly. I stood a few feet from the door still looking into the dark for the source of the voice.

Scratching. Where from? Slowly a ball of light appeared and a table came into view, then some hands, the glowing intensified and a figure came into view. Who was it? Was he going to hurt me? A large, rough looking man with a facial scar sat looking at me. His hair lined with grey. A hat lay on the table with a few black feather spouting form the rim.

He rises from the table causing huge shadows to emerge on the wall behind him.

'Didn't ye hear me boy? What're ye doing here?' he asks again. I can't seem to find my words.

'I-I needed s-somewhere to st-stay.' I mumbled. He looked at me as if to determine the truth to what I'd said.

'what's ya name?' he asks

'Jake.' He gives me the same look as though he thinks I'm lying.

'Rigel.' He introduces himself.

He doesn't say another word but leaves the table and crosses the room into more darkness every step creaking as he went. Another light starts to glow and I see a small make shift kitchen of one portable hob and kettle alongside a storage cooler. In silence he makes hot drinks and places them both on the table. He offers me one. Motions me to sit with him. I do so, more out of fear than anything else.

'So why're ye here, Jake? The truth.' He asks with a sigh. With a shaky voice I tell him about the trouble I'd been in and how I ran away so my mum didn't need to worry about me. He listens without interrupting until I've finished.

'Running away will only make ya Ma worry about ya more, d'you know that?' he asks. 'Poor lady, she'd probably be running mad looking for ya.' I look at the floor ashamed as it dawns on me the truth in his words. 'Stay here for tonight. We'll decide what t' do in t' morning.' He gives me a blanket and somewhere to sleep. I hardly slept though.

I didn't go home the next day. Or the day after that. I stayed with Rigel, somehow we built a friendship and he took me under his wing. He told me about his past. How he'd gotten into trouble for burglary when he was young. He was arrested throughout his 20s but an altercation, as he called it, got out of hand. He was convicted and sent to prison and he had carried on thieving after his release. He's been to prison a few times.

I helped him fix his aircraft once. Just as I always wanted my father to do. I told him about my father too. Rigel kept me out of trouble, took the blame for me when I got caught stealing. He even got me to return home, but I visited him often. He was the dad I never had. I even started calling him dad. We have a running joke between us:

'Dad!' I'd say.

'I think that's called a faux pas.' He'd say.

'Exactly!' I'd reply and we'd laugh at the play on words.

Eventually I turned 18. Mum started getting sick. She had tests at the hospital and found she had cancer. Treatment didn't work. It was then that Rigel drove home the reality.

'Ye need to make ya Ma proud before she passes, Jake.' He told me. 'Don't end up like me. You still have a chance to make something of yourself. Show her that you can.' He was right. I had to. I managed to enrol at the Minors Military Unit and I worked harder than I ever had before. They offered me a conditional place in the Fleet if I helped them with a case. I was all for helping them until I found out it was a case against Rigel. I refused to help them imprison him again. I lost my place and got offered a place in the mechanics sector. After that I kept my visits to Rigel few and far between. I knew they'd try and catch him out and possibly use me to do it.

My mum's condition got worse and she grew frail and weak.

I visited her in the hospital. I told her what had happened. She always knew about Rigel. I told her the first time I went back home after running away. She understood.

'I'm *so* proud of you, Jacob.' She managed to get out. She touched my face. Her hand was like ice.

'I understand why you didn't give up Rigel.' She said through laboured breaths. 'I love you. My sweet boy.' I hugged her once last time as she passed not long after that.

Rigel came to her funeral. He stayed hidden obviously. He decided to pay his respects after everyone had gone. I didn't have anyone else. With my mum gone he was the only family I have.

If anything ever became of me and Lina, I think my mum would've liked her. I'm so confused. She kissed me back and then pushed me away like she'd touched fire.

I didn't see Lina at all today. She wasn't in our room. I made my way to the hidden garage I took her to last night. The door was already open. There she was. She turned in surprise as I closed the door. Her arms full of aluminium. The floor was covered in it.

'It's lighter than steel.' She offered. 'For the frame. I spent all day at the scrap sector collecting it.' I can't quite believe what I'm hearing. I just look from the metal to her. 'I'm sorry.' She says. I almost laugh. She knows how to make an apology matter. All day in scrap just to help me. I smile at her as I take the aluminium from her arms and pull her into my arms and held her tight.

'Thank you.' I whispered to her.

Truth

We stayed up the next few nights making the frame. We worked together to weld and shape the pieces together. I, being use to the tools welded the pieces together with ease and speed whereas Lina, being new to it all still, takes time and care in what she does. No easy task when we have to make it as aerodynamic as possible. We did it. I welded the last piece to the door and looked around. She was fast asleep on the floor. I placed my jacket over her. I never really got it back since I gave it to her about a week ago. I lead down next to her and stared at her. She looks so peaceful. Carefully I put my arm around her and drift off into a deep sleep.

I woke at some point in the night to find Jake sleeping next to me, arm around my waist. He must be exhausted from working on the craft for, what feels like, days on end. Looking at him makes almost every worry I have fade away. Gently, I sweep some of his thick brown hair from his face. I cuddle into him and pull the jacket over him, so we share, with my arm around him I drift off back to sleep.

When we woke the next morning we spend some time lying there having pillow talk and we decided to test the craft that night. I'm so excited! I really hope it works.

That evening after a day of welding, part replacements etc. I pack a backpack with some food, drink a couple blankets. It's meant to get cold tonight. I secretly pack an extra toolbox, just in case.

Well, you never know what could go wrong. I meet Jake downstairs. He greets me with a big cheesy grin.

'Alright?' he asks as I make my way to the craft.

'Quite excited to be honest. You?' I tell him as I throw the backpack into the back of the cockpit.

'Yes. And a bit nervous. It's never flown before.' He admits taking a step back beside me as we take a moment to admire our hard work.

'First time for everything.' I say, breaking the moment and climbing into my seat. 'Ready?' I smile at him. The excitement almost spilling over. If this craft flies then maybe I can go and search for Lyra. Be done with the pain. Be done with the internal conflict. When I have Lyra back I'll know then if my feelings are real or displaced. Everything I feel is like a physical pain.

He smiles back at me and jumps into the pilots seat. Seat belts on. Reinforced doors open. It's now or never. I squeeze his shoulder form my seat behind him. He squeezes my hand back.

'Let's go.' He says before taking a breath to steady his nerve. He presses the start button and the buttons in the cockpit light up as the engine comes to life. I'm nervous. My breath catches in my throat. Jake presses some buttons and gently pulls the steering wheel. Shakily, it rises into the air.

'It works!' I exclaim, laughing in relief. I can see Jake is relieved as well. Now for the real test, how far will it go? Jake steers the craft towards the exit and next thing I know we're flying, gaining speed as we climb further into the night sky. On the way up, Jake makes the craft do loops and spins. It was thrilling. I think I let out a scream at some point. We speed through the air swerving round buildings making zigzags as we head towards the stars. This isn't some careful first test flight like I would've done. Jake decides to be daring. Why just do a basic test when you can have fun with it like this? I want to fly in this craft again. I've never known anything so exciting. So addictive. So...fun!

We slow down a bit as we get above the city's skyline. It looks so pretty from up here.

'Look up.' Jake says half turning to me, snapping me out of my trance on the city before going back to concentrating on driving. I glance up and my breath escapes my body. I can't believe what I'm seeing. A massive mass of stars emitting a multitude of different colours stretches out above us. Pinks, purples, blues and whites all mixed together. It's absolutely beautiful. I wrap my arms over the seat and round Jake.

'It's amazing.' I breathe.

'That's the Oriana Nebula. Only seen once a year, providing the sky is clear.' He tells me.

'I've never heard of it.' I tell him. I recognise the name belonging to my 5x great grandmother. She was the new love of King Wolf after coming here.

'Apparently it was named after Queen Oriana after it being seen for the first time just after they married or something.'

'I never knew that.' I feel a little hurt I was never told about this nebula in my studies.

'Where do you want to go?' he asks changing the subject. I look out over the skyline again. The buildings outlined by the luminous blue sand by the coast. In the distance I see the island, only visible by the blue sand that outlines it.

'There.' I point to the island putting my arm in his line of view before sitting back. He steers so we're heading towards it. I don't know why it was never given a name. It's always been 'The Island'. I feel guilty though. I knew I had to get out of him what I could about Rigel.

We make great time. The craft goes faster than I expected. We sail over the water going a few miles to the island. I find a large enough area of sand to land on the far side of the island facing away from the city. I ease up the acceleration to make the landing and we land safely.

Lina jumps out almost as soon as the overhead door opens backpack in tow. What did she have in there?

'It certainly flies well.' She says walking away from the craft.

'Thanks to the aluminium.' I try to subtly compliment her as I catch up to her. She stops and looks up to the sky. Constellations and far off planets looking like tiny white dots in the distance. We can't see the Oriana from here. When I look back at her she's already looking at me. My heart skips.

'Here looks good.' She says as she looks away quick taking the backpack off and dropping it on the sand. She pulls out a Bio Orb and walks off picking up driftwood and kindling before bringing it back. She makes a pile and somehow in the dark she makes a fire. I couldn't see how in the dark. She amazes me. She's so fragile at times yet she manages to do something I never expected of her. She pulls out blankets, lies one out on the sand and motions for me to sit. I do so like an obedient pet. She continues to pull out two more blankets for us. It was surprisingly cold for early September.

We sit for a bit, blankets round us, by the heat of the fire. The shape of the island curves out further down the beach. The blue light showing the way. I can make out silhouettes of trees and large boulders stranded up ahead, all worn smooth with time. The sound of the water as it laps against the shore has a way of making me feel relaxed.

She just stares out into the distance, her green eyes intense. What's going on in her mind?

'What are you thinking?' I decide to just come straight out and ask her.

'I just miss my family.' She half smiles trying to make out like it isn't hurting her.

'Same.' I say suddenly feeling like I'm alone in the world. All I have is Lina and Rigel.

'Don't you have anybody?' she asks 'brothers? Sisters? Aunties?'

'Sort of...' I begin. 'But he's not blood.' She looks at me expectantly, waiting for me to continue. 'There's someone I've known since I was about 15/16. He's the dad I never had. He took me in in a way.' I confess. 'We always did things that I wanted my father to do. Things like fixing the family aircraft together. I don't get to see him very often though.'

'He sounds like a good person. What's his name?' I say. *'This is it'* my mind tells me. I need to get him to talk about Rigel. I *have* to string him along. I don't want to but if it's going to be between him and Lyra – it's Lyra.

'He is a good person. Had a tough past mind but he's a good person.'

'You can't always judge someone on their past mistakes.' I tell him. He looks surprised. He know I mean him. He's told me about his past with theft and trespassing etc. looking at him now I can't help but feel emotional. This guy is so kind and I have to be horrible to him. My heart aches. It feels like it could give up on me at any moment. I can't go on feeling like this. I know it'll only get worse first though.

'What's his name?' I ask again. He hesitates. I can see in his eyes that he's trying to decide if he can trust me enough. I hate that I'm going to have to break that trust.

'I never met my mother.' I disclose to him. I hope my honesty will be the branch needed for him to trust me enough to talk about it.

'What happened to her?' he asks. A new tie coming to life as we shared stories of relatable events and finding understanding.

'I don't know.' I reveal. 'I have no actual memories. I have a picture in my head of me standing by my parents' bed looking at her. I don't know if it's real or if I made it up though.' I sigh. 'Over the years, it's like the features have blurred, so I don't even know who it is.' I continue to tell him how I once asked my dad where my mother was and he looked at me with big eyes and pretended he hadn't heard me. 'I don't know if she's alive or dead. If she's alive then where is she?' a moment of silence passes. Only a moment but it felt like ages.

One of his strong arms wraps around my shoulder and her pulls me close, resting his head on mine.

'Rigel.' He answers eventually. 'His name is Rigel.' I look up at him. He has my full attention. Now is my chance.

'Why don't you see him?' I ask. I need as much information as I can.

'He's been in trouble with the Fleet before. They're trying to find him. I can't give up on him. He's never given up on me.' He looks at the sand with painful memories of being given up on flashing through his mind. My heart feels like it's physically tearing in two.

'He's the only family I have left.' He confesses. That was it my heart broke. That familiar prickle in my eyes as new tears began to form. *Stay focused* I tell myself. I've been trying to tell myself all along that he isn't important enough to break down over...but I always knew it was a lie. He continues.

'I always wanted a family' he says, looking back out over the sea. 'Meet someone. Settle down. Have kids. But how can I be a dad when I never really had one myself?' these blasted tears are threatening to fall now. The truth suffocating me. I can't tell him. I mustn't. I try my best to swallow the truth lump that has formed before answering him.

'I don't know what you're like with children but I think you'd make a great dad one day.' I tell him honestly. He turns to me. I can tell he doesn't believe me.

'What's wrong?' he asks seeing my glazed eyes.

'Just the talk of family.' I wasn't lying. Gently he takes my hand. It feels nice. His rough warm hands in mine. My heart fills with pain all over again.

'I fear-' he pauses. 'I fear I will walk out on them. Just like my father did to me.'

'I don't think you will.' He looks at me again, his eyes full of hope. The look of someone who desperately needs to be told what they need to hear. 'You know what it feels like to just be left. No explanation. No apologies and he never came back. It's one thing separating from the mum but to leave a child with nothing.' I take a breath. 'You know what that feels like. You know how it hurts. I don't believe you'd put anyone through that, especially your own children.' My voice falters on me as I put my thoughts into words. 'At least once in your life a Being will hurt you.' I can hardly get my words out. 'You just don't expect that Being to be some you love.'

He pulls me in tighter. I meant every word. The tears were down my cheek. I don't want to lie to him anymore. I can't make him give up his family. The pain is too much now. I have to stand up and distance myself from him. I'm shaking. I feel sick. I feel his hands on my shoulders as he tries to comfort me but I shake him off. This annoys him.

'Why do you hold me at arm's length?! Why do you push me away?!' His voice raised.

Anything I do will be wrong and hurt someone but I can't do it anymore. I'm going to be that Being. The Being that hurts him.

'It's the only way I can protect myself.' I yell back. 'I'm not the person you think I am, Jake.'

'Just when I think you're letting me in you push me away.' He yells back at me. The tears from me fall thick and fast now. Can't this be over? Can't I just have Lyra back and we can sort this out?! 'I can tell you're hiding something from me. I'm not stupid, Lina! Let me help you!'

That's it. The truth comes out. Every single detail. How my real name is Adelina. How my daughter is missing. How the Fleet are looking for Rigel. That he's the lead suspect because of evidence. That I wasn't supposed to be involved and how because of lack of soldiers, I was appointed to be a Spare. To get information out of him. How I have developed feeling for him but they could be displaced because of the state I'm in mentally over my baby. How I hate that I have to lie to him and use him.

'All I want is my baby back!' I finish with as I fall down the sand in hysteria. Crying loudly.

I can't believe what I'm hearing. She used me. She's trying to get Rigel. I just admitted to her how important he is to me. I turn away from her as I try to take it all in. How could she? She knew I had feelings for her and she still used me. For what?! To follow a lead?! One I know is rubbish! He wouldn't do that! I know him! He wouldn't. All this and for what?! To find her child?!

That's when it clicked...her child. I run my hands through my hair. I feel like I've been hit with a ton of bricks. She's a mother just looking for her child in the only way she thought she could. The only option she was given. I know if it was my child I'd want to be the one out there looking. I'd jump at any opportunity to help find them. That's exactly what she was doing. Trying to find her missing child. She's desperate.

I look at her curled up in the sand. The hurt doesn't go away but the anger melts away. It's replaced with empathy. This poor woman. No other choice.

She admitted feelings for me but she doesn't know if it's real. I get that...I think. I'll admit, that hurts too. My feelings being so strong and hers being questionable.

I take a minute to think. Rigel won't have her. I *know* that. Kidnapping isn't anything like what he's done before. I don't believe he's the suspect.

She looks so fragile. The pain that's been held within now obvious to see. It all makes sense now. Her not wanting to get out of bed. Her terrified look the first time I met her. Her pulling away from kissing me. She was hurting but not wanting to hurt me either while at the same time just wanting to find her child. How did she hide all those feelings?

I make my way over to her and pull her close once more. This time she hugs me back. My trust in her might be damaged but my feelings for her were stronger than ever.

'I'm going to need to build trust up with you again...' I whisper to her 'but you're not doing this alone anymore.' She looks up at me with the same wide eyed look as the first time I laid eyes on her, only this time, they were full of hope. 'I'll take you to see Rigel. He didn't do this. I know it but I'll help you find her.' I hold her tight. 'I promise.'

She holds me tighter crying with relief. My chest aches for her. I know the truth now. We can start fresh.

After a while she pulls away from me. Her eyes red and face blotchy from crying. Without a word, she kisses me. Gently at first. I don't stop her. I kiss her back. Her face is warm against mine, if a little wet too. We kiss again and again getting more and more passionate. I slowly, in the moment, run my hands under her top. She doesn't stop me. Instead, she starts to undo my belt. I kiss her neck as I take her top off and we continue to strip we get back to the blankets and I held her body close to mine, feeling her warmth, as we had sex by the fire.

Rigel

We got back to the room at some point last night. We had sex again in the room. I love the way his body felt against mine. I didn't want it to end I couldn't get enough of him. I woke up in his bed. He wasn't next to me. I pull my mess of hair out of my face as I sit up, keeping the duvet around me. I feel weird. I press my head against the window looking out over the residing buildings. The sun is warm on my face through the glass.

I make my way to the chest of draws and find out the children's' book I'd been hiding under my trousers. Looking at it I know how I feel as I lean against the window again. Happy. Happiness and hope. I feel closer to Lyra than I have for weeks. I hold it to my chest hugging it tight. I feel calm. Content.

'Morning.' Jake says when he comes through the door. I can't help but smile at him as butterflies danced inside me. He kisses the side of my head as he wraps his arms around me from behind and I lean into him still looking out of the window.

'What've you got there?' he asks noticing the book. I let him take it. He lets out a small laugh 'My mum use to read these to me.' His smile fades. 'Is this Lyra's?' I nod. He puts his arms around me and kisses my head again. I love how he can make me feel so calm in a terrible situation. He's promised to help me find her. He doesn't even know her and he's made this promise. My head tells me I love him but I won't tell him just in case it isn't so. I've messed him around enough.

'Get dressed.' He says breaking away. 'We'll leave in half an hour.' He looks thoughtfully at the book. No doubt memories of his mum were connected to it. The same memories I had with my daughter. He walks back to the door and places it in a backpack that I hadn't even seen there. Looking up at me he sees the confused look on my face.

'When we find her, it might be nice if she has something familiar, y'know.' The fact that he even considered that for her made my heart stop for a moment. Turning away to find some clothes I can't wipe the smile off my face.

Half an hour later we were in the craft, flying south over the city. We know Stevens will be angry at us for not turning up this morning but I don't think either of us care.

We leave the city behind us and fly over vast areas of green and the occasional village. We fly over a large and winding river for about half an hour or more. I see large rocks line the edge of the river, separating the bank from the thin of the forest. I can just make out the tiny silver ribbons that line the tiny waves and disappear as they crash into bank. I know by that that we're flying over the Silver Forest, known for its Silver looking waters and silver hues in winter. I've never been to this part of Vulcadon. To be fair, I've never really left the city.

I'm nervous. He's taking me to meet Rigel. The person I've believe for weeks to be the one who has taken Lyra. Jake swears he hasn't. I don't know what or who to believe.

I fly over the familiar route. One I've taken many times before. After a while I see the usual spot on the bank where there's a clearing on the edge of the tree. I set the craft down in the clearing with a bit of a bump-it's only the second flight I'm still getting used to it.

I help Lina out of the craft.

'This way.' I lead her by the hand to a path hidden by overgrown thorns. Moving them out the way reveals a path, worn by time and hidden by towering trees. Sun rays filter down through the trees. I can hear the sounds of the wildlife nearby, hidden from view.

I'm accustomed to everything around me. Its home. The rustle of the leaves overhead and even the dull thud of our feet on the path feels welcoming. I feel so light and free here. I turn to Lina, walking backwards for a minute. She looks scared.

'It's ok, y'know.' I try to reassure her. 'He isn't a bad person.'

'I'll take your word for it.' she forces a smile. I can't even imagine what must be going through her head right now. I abruptly stop walking forcing her to stop in her tracks. I try to come up with something to say but there's nothing. Nothing at all I can do to make this any easier.

'I'm afraid.' She reveals shyly.

'Why?' I ask genuinely confused.

'I don't know this guy. What if he gets mad and yells at me? What if he refuses to help because I think he might have taken Lyra?' I take her hands entwining our fingers and rest my forehead against hers. How could I forget that it's me who knows him? It's me who knows how he'll react. Not her. Stupid bloody idiot.

'It's not far now.' I say pulling away. What else am I meant to say to that? Oh don't worry its ok because I know him?

That's not going to make her feel any better. I have to let her get her own impression of him.

I resume leading her down the path. Before us a gorge revealed itself from behind the tress. I walk a little further down the path.

'We're here.' I say unable to hide my happiness at finding the place. She looks up at the side of the gorge confused. 'This way.' I smile at her. Just behind the curve of the gorge is a cave. One of those 'blink and you'll miss it' ones. The kind that gets discovered hundreds of years after the others. We stand in front of what looks like part of the rock face. I raise my hand and knock 3 fast taps followed by 2 slow then 3 fast. Almost immediately the rock face moves. It slides to the right slotting itself between layers of stone.

'Like it?' I ask Lina indicating the door. 'Rigel and I built it when we came across this place.'

She looks stunned, unable to get any words out.

How did they 'come across' a place like this?! It's so well protected that you could easily miss it.

This was it. I'm trying to prepare myself for coming face to face with Rigel. Mentally going over every possible scenario in my head. I grip Jake's hand a bit tighter. He squeezes back.

He guides me down what seems like a never ending tunnel leading deep into the cave. As we get further from the entrance darkness enthrals us until I'm blind as it dawns on me that I'm going into a dark cave with a man I've known a matter of weeks to see a convicted criminal about the possible whereabouts of my daughter. I could be walking to my death right now. I grab my Cariopius from my pocket, just in case. I can't see where I'm stepping or see Jake in front of me. I can only feel his hand in mine. All my trust is in Jake now. The only thing I can concentrate on right now is follow.

Suddenly, as my eyes adjust, I can see a dull glow in the distance. I feel like I'm being pulled now. I don't know if it's Jake's excitement to see an old friend or my apprehension.

These last few seconds feel like a lifetime as we make a last turn and enter the room the light is coming from. It opens up onto a small, dusty room. Before us a table sits. Upon it lies a cutlass and a mini Nysa. To one side bottles of water and a metal bowl I presume is for washing up. A hole in the wall filled with food and a cloth to cover it making a fridge using the coolness that comes with the depth. In front of it a large human stands before it. I already know who it's Rigel without him even turning around which he does as we enter the room. He's taller than I imagined. My heart races so fast it threatens to burst out of my chest. I didn't dare breath. Black feathers fall entwined into his dreaded hair. The scar by his eye standing out a mile, even in this dull light. I can't move. I feel like a child in one of those 'if I don't move he won't see me' situations that defy all logic. My mind races with thoughts of him killing me. I'm over reacting. The logical part of me knows this but I can't stop myself. Conflicted between running away and staying to get the information I desperately need.

He straightens himself out adjusting to the sight of us before bearing a huge toothy grin.

'Jake!' he exclaims almost too loud in this small stone room.

'Dad!' Jake exclaims back giving this frightening looking man a hug.

'I think that's called a faux pas' Rigel half laughs.

81

'Exactly!' Jake replies with the same half laugh and grin. My fears seem to melt away as I see the happiness on Jake's face. The delight and relaxed atmosphere now making me feel I can let my guard down a bit. They chat and quickly catch up as I linger in the doorway. I've never seen Jake this happy. Part of me really hope Rigel had nothing to do with it now. I couldn't bear Jake being crushed if he got sent back to prison.

The joy I feel at seeing my dad is unexplainable. The joy tinged with sadness I try to ignore each time as I know he isn't my real father.

He's been away recently. Got back a few days ago he tells me.

'Got me self into a wee situation, boy but I tell ya I'm alright. The other guy got a bit of a broken face mind ya.' He says. That means he's been caught thieving again but he doesn't want to give me the details. He looks up to the door and sees Lina loitering. Her instinct makes her automatically hide as soon as he looks at her.

'Who's this then, Jake?' he asks. 'Ya brought a girl with ya?' I know he's only being cautious. This place has been a haven for him since we found it. He's trying to protect his sanctuary. Immediately I jump in to defend them both.

'It's ok.' I address them both standing between them as common ground. 'She with me.' I tell Rigel. I turn to Lina and hold my hand out. She sweeps strands of her hair that have come loose from her ponytail out of her face as she carefully comes into the small room and takes my hand.

'What's this? New girlfriend, Jake?' Rigel half jokes. Last time I saw him he was on about me, in his words, 'find ya self a girl and settle down boy. Nothing like a good woman to help ya through life.' He's always been the type of person who never took anything too seriously unless it was necessary.

'Not exactly.' I admit. 'It's a long story.' I motion to the table for us to sit down. Rigel's happy demeanour suddenly becomes serious.

'Ye haven't gone and got this girl pregnant, have ya?'

'NO! No. it's more serious than that.' I say firmly shooting down the idea quickly.

'Better put t' kettle on then.' Straightening up, realising just *how* grave the situation was.

We gather around the small table, all with our teas. Lina holding on to her like her life depended on it. She looks tired, delicate with her hair in her face again. I reveal everything. Tell him the whole story. Well what I knew from what Lina had told me. He sits silently listening to every word as it hits him how severe it is for all of us. Every now and then he glances at her and she sinks further down into her chair. I hold her hand in support. Once I finish filling him in he takes a moment to mull it all over. I know he's shocked by the revelation that he's the main suspect. He doesn't tend to show his emotions.

'I'm sorry, love.' He looks up at Lina. 'I haven't got ya babby.'

Pain crosses her face as she crumbles into tears. Her last hope gone.

That was it. My last hope destroyed in 5 words. What am I meant to do now? An intense pain torn through my chest as my heart was ripped out. It might have hurt less if someone actually had. Jake tries to comfort me but I push him away. I need to be alone. The scrape of the chairs legs against the cave floor echoed as I got up from the table and left. I hear Rigel tell Jake to 'let her go, boy. She needs a minute.'

I stumbled into another room once again light by the dull orbs dimmed by the lack of natural sunlight they needed to soak up in order to shine bright. With my eyesight blurred by tears I slump in the corner. Hugging my knees as close to my chest as I could get, my lack of flexibility causing cramp in my upper leg, I ignored that pain and allowed myself to be consumed by the unbearable pain I was currently experiencing.

I lose time as I wallow in my self-pity. Immersed in my hatred for the Being that took my precious daughter, angry over the fact there is nothing else to go on. I'm disappointed that the work I've put into finding her lead to two innocent Beings being hurt especially as I care deeply for one of them. I'm furious with the Fleet for not being told anything since Costello's 'investigation'. I'm inconsolable over the fact that even I couldn't protect my own child. And now she's gone. Forever.

Eventually the tears don't fall as fast and I'm calmer although empty inside and unable to determine what in Lucinesri I was supposed to do now.

I shiver as a light breeze tickles the curve of my neck. I look round in the direction it came from and saw another doorway. A door means another way out. I need fresh air to clear my head. Pulling myself up I follow the breeze into the dark room and then the next one in which I could see a sliver of sunlight shining through.

Stepping through the exit I'm momentarily visually impaired. My sore eyes adjust to the new brightness.

Grass spreads out underfoot and a silver lake twinkles like diamonds. Star shaped flowers bloomed boldly from the nearby hedges. The crisp breeze fills my lungs renewing some of the life that had drained from me just minutes earlier. Small webbed winged creatures flap around high above me. Trees where the branches bridge and interlink overhead. Only sun rays can filter through hiding this entire bit of land from view above. I can hear songs from some local creatures but I can't see them hiding from my view. This place was astonishing. So perfect, so natural, so…safe. Despite my feelings being raw, I felt strangely at peace here although I was still crying. This is the perfect place to clear my head I decide as I sit by the edge of the lake, dip my fingers in causing it to ripple outwards.

I lean against the side, biting my thumbnail as I tried desperately to think of a solution. Rigel is watching me from the other side of the small room. His arms crossed but with one hand on his chin I can't make out if he's thinking of an answer or waiting for me to get angry and shout it all out like I had done in the past to get it all off my chest. I hadn't done that in years though.

'There's got to be another way.' I declare as I start pacing. I can't keep still we need a solution for Lina. 'Help me! She's hurting. She needs to find her.'

'You really care for her, don't ya Jake.' An annoying know-it-all smile crept across his face. I stop pacing and shift my weight instead. I can't bring myself to look at him.

'Well, yeah.' I reveal just like an embarrassed kid trying to deny something to a parent.

'D'ya love her?'

'What's it to you?' I joke but I give it away when I can't force myself not to smile about it. 'I'm not going to say that. I haven't known her long.'

I can't say I'm in love with her but I know how I feel. I look towards the doorway she ran through a while ago longing to go and be with her. Rigel comes and stands by me his steps heavy.

'So what is it about her?' I stop and look at him. His arms crossed and an expectant look on his face. 'You found a girl more broken than you and you want to fix her-'

'NO!' it's not the same as past relationships. 'She the opposite of me. She's cautious and grounded. She balances me.' I go to leave.

'Now, ya listen to me boy.' He tells me taking me by the shoulders and getting eye level with me.

'ye and I both know how t' most precious tings can be gone in a second.' I know he's talking about the woman he was going to marry in his teens. The only girl he ever loved.

'Don't make t' same mistake as I did. Ya know how ya feel. Go with it! Don't leave it t' long. I see t' way ya look at her. It's the same way I used to look at Mel.' Hope filled me as I turned again to the door. 'Now develop a back bone and go and tell her!' I went to run, to tell her then and there that I love her and I would be with her through it. I wouldn't leave her to deal with this alone. I went to go but Rigel's strong hand pulled me back by my arm.

'Just one more ting.' He says stopping me. He leans in and whispers to me. 'Why are the fleet investigating a missing kiddie case? That's not there jurisdiction.'

It dawned on me that I didn't know. I hadn't thought about it.

The Lake

The rays that managed to snake down through the twisted branches warmed my back and cool water glittered. I am calmer now. The pain still very real of course. I want to block it all out. I want to forget but at the same time I don't. The memories filled me. The love and pride still as fresh as the moment they happened. Her infectious laugh ringing in my ears. One of the webbed winged creatures perched beside me to drink from the lake. I remained still so I didn't scare it off. It looked up and me, titled its head from side to side before flying off.

'I'll talk to her. Wait here.' a rough voice says, I whirl round and see Rigel making his way towards the lake while Jake waited by the doorway. I could tell by his demeanour that he wanted a serious chat with me. I don't feel scared this time.

His heavy steps get to me and he rigidly takes a seat on the boulder a few feet away.

'Beautiful, isn't it?' he indicates the wonderful scenery around me breaking the ice. I nod. 'This here is my sanctuary.' He tells me looking out at the lake, the light looking like glitter in his eyes.

'This is my home. Sacred to me this is.' I say nothing. 'Look, love.' I turn only my head. 'I won't lie to ya. I won't say it'll be ok. I can't imagine what ya going through.' He sounds honest.

'I never had kids of me own.' I remain quiet. Where is he going with this?

'I was going to get married once.' A small, pained smile flickers as he draws on a painful memory. 'Met a beautiful girl when I was 17. Love of my life. Knew she was t' one. The one I was going to have a future with. A home, kids, t' lot' His voice and face light up as he talks about her. 'We were going t' get married as soon as we were 18.' His face saddens. 'I lost her though. She were flying in a craft with her family.' I listen intently. The rest of the world fades away. He sounded heartbroken even now. I guess the pain of true love never goes away.

'Something went wrong.' He continues. 'It started smoking. Caught fire. It exploded and crashed into the sea. Everyone died.' I see a tear come to his eye. I'm sure just for that moment he was back to that day. Breaking away from the thought he clears his throat.

'How awful.' I answer once again unable to find relevant words of comfort. 'It sounds horrible.'

'Aye, that it were, love.' He confirms. 'My pain felt unbearable but yours must be a hundred times worse.' He wasn't comforting me, just trying to show I wasn't alone in knowing unforgiving pain.

'I'm not going to say that I'm sorry for your loss. That won't bring her back. That's just something people say when they don't know how to react.'

'I respect your honesty, love.'

I take in this large, scary looking man. I remember the hate that burned inside me the first time I saw him on the hologram. I believed him to be a monster but this moment he shared with me showed me he really wasn't.

'I'm sorry though.' I confess after a moment.

'For what?' I confessed what I had believed about him and my impression of him now. He let out a small laugh.

'Don't worry about it. I get that a lot.' I smile at him feeling like I'd made a friend. I go back to admiring the landscape, the world suddenly back around us as I feel the warmth again.

'Don't think me rude, what evidence is there, that puts me in that room?' I turn to him again, go to speak then stop. I became fully aware that I didn't know. I know there was evidence but I didn't know what that evidence is. I told him so and wanted the ground to swallow me up as it emerged that I had my sights set on Rigel without any solid reason to. I was told he was the suspect and that there was evidence but I didn't know any more than that really. It's no wonder Costello was reluctant to have me on the case. Emotionally stable me would've found all this out before going in head first. How can I be so stupid?

I apologise profusely. He says its ok and he understands but how can he? I'm so angry at myself.

'Anyway.' He changes the subject. 'What I really want to talk to ya about.' He straightens up and glances over towards the rock face. I glance to and see Jake still standing there, waiting patiently.

'I see t' way he looks at you.' He says still looking at Jake. I flush red. 'He's had a hard time. I don't want him hurt.' I know what he's getting at.

'I don't want to hurt him again.' I answered simply without making eye contact. 'I never intended to hurt him in the first place. 'I didn't plan on developing feelings for him. He knows that I'm not sure if they're real or...' what's the word? I feel like

I'm choking. 'Forced so I feel something other than pain.' Rigel sits watching me. Listening.

'Ya don't know him like I do, love.' He says after a moment. 'I understand where ya coming from, don't get me wrong. He's been hurt enough.' He looks thoughtful for a moment. 'Let me be honest with ya.' He gets level with me. 'He's the son I never had. The son I like to believe Mell and I would've had. I just want him to be happy.'

I respect his concern. I see why Jake thinks of him as his dad. I wish I could be the person they both want.

'I'm not going to make any promises.' I tell him truthfully. 'I've got enough to deal with.'

We quickly go quiet as we notice Jake walking towards us. My instinct was to look away and pretend to be casual but the atmosphere gave it away. If he noticed, he didn't say anything. He sits down beside me and slips his hand in mine. I feel accountable for all his hurt. With the topic of conversation being about him and how I can't promise to love him I want to pull away but I also want the comfort. I pray that I'm not using his kind heartedness for my selfish need.

'I promised I'd help her.' Jake tells Rigel once settled on the grass. He ran his thumb over mine. 'I don't know what to do though. Where do we go from here?'

No one answered. Another moments that felt like forever dragged out. Where do we go from here? How am I meant to find her now? She could be anywhere.

We decided to stay there that night. Neither of us were prepared to deal with Stevens' wrath. She's hardly said a word since her Rigel spoke to her. I feel so helpless. Like always I'm useless. What can you do when the only thing that can make it better is an impossibility? I find out pillows and duvets to make the bed in. what has always been, my room. She helps me on autopilot. I can smell the stew Rigel is cooking up. She's a shell. She's there in person but not in soul. When we finished shaking out the duvet and pulling it over the bed she crossed her arms and stayed still. Personally, I'm still hurt from last night. The part of me that tries to steer clear of any kind of pain and lies wanted to run away from her, only this time it wasn't winning. Running is the last thing I wanted to do. The stronger part of me shouted to hold her until the pain went away. I made my way round the bed and enveloped her. Without fighting she rested herself into me.

'Talk to me.' I beg. I feel her arms unfold and slither round my waist.

'Wha-what if no one ever finds her.' I feel her tense up. 'What if she's-' she breaks down in tears on my shoulder. She didn't need to finish that sentence. I hold her tighter. She didn't need to say anything now. I knew she just admitted her worse fear. It doesn't bear thinking about.

'Don't even think that.' I try to soothe her. 'We'll think of something.'

She titled her head to look up at me. Her eyes full of pain. My heart betraying me and started to race. She kisses me. I rest my forehead on hers. Selfishly I wish there wasn't this 'does she? Doesn't she?' hanging over us. I want her. I pull her in tighter. She kisses me again and again leaning into me so much I lose balance, landing on the bed. She climbs on top of me. Something inside me tells me to stop. I want her but it isn't right. She's hurting and I don't want to take advantage. I roll to the side making her fall off of me and quickly get up.

'What did you do that for?' she asks angry, shaking, her breath coming in rasps as she tried to control it.

'Lina, you're hurting. It wouldn't be right.'

'Just make me feel something different!' she pleads. I say no. her shoulders fall. It breaks my heart to see her this way. I'd love to see her happy. What was she like before all of this happened?

'You make me feel safe.' She says calmly. I make her feel safe. Me? She needs me. I pull her into a bear hug only letting go when she pulls away.

I leave her on the bed after she said she was tired. She hasn't had much sleep, really, since the first night I met her. She'd always stay awake for hours and never want to wake in the morning. I promised to wake her when food was ready.

Making my way to the kitchen I slump down into a chair suddenly exhausted. I let out an exasperated sigh as I run my hands through my hair. I don't think I've ever felt so many emotions in less than 24 hours.

'Ya alright boy?' Rigel asked stirring the stew and I ignored the rumbling in my stomach.

'Didn't know I could feel this much.' I confess. 'I'm not use to it but I don't want it to go either. I just wish there was something-anything-I could do.'

He pulls up the chair opposite me making the legs scratch against the rock floor.

'Jake.' He gets my attention. 'I been thinking. Is it t' be believed that it's something t' do with her family?'

'I think so.'

'What if it isn't?' I sit up. What's he getting to? He goes to speak again when we both see a figure appear in the door. Lina. I guess she couldn't bring herself to sleep.

'What do you mean?' she asks bringing herself into the conversation. Rigel kicks out a chair for her.

'I mean, what if it's not you they're trying to get to?' Lina and I are both confused. Why wouldn't it be to do with her family?

'Lina?' he looks directly at her. 'Why are the Fleet involved?' I fear her answer. She takes a breath. I feel my heart in my chest.

'I'm Princess Adelina Ophelia Chandra Lune. I'm also Second in Command of the Fleet.'

Silence. We both stunned. What on this world was happening?! Yesterday I was just a mechanic with feelings for a girl with secrets. Now, I'm sat on at a table in a cave with my dad and a princess in a situation that has just got a lot more complicated.

Neither of us say anything for a moment as we take it all in. in the end Rigel decides to carry on with what he originally planned to before this revelations.

'Right. Ok.' He clears his throat. 'What if it's me? What if someone is trying t' frame me t' get back at me for something I've done in t' past?'

'Enough to kidnap a child?' I ask sceptical.

'Enough to want me put away for life or even dead.' It's true. An offence like this can end up with a death sentence if not a life sentence.

'But who would want to get back at you that bad?' I ask.

'There's a few that'd want t' get me back.' He thinks hard for a minute.

'There's a few names that comes t' mind but most left t' city years ago. Some died. T' only one that's still in t' city is Rapha Blagden. T can't be him thought. he's been inside for t' last 5 years.'

'Are you sure?' Lina asks, grasping at straws.

'Aye. I'm sure.' Rigel sounds disheartened. 'I put him there.'

I let out an infuriated sigh. What now? Are there any other options? Have we missed something? Is there another way to look at this?

Out of worry I turn to Lina, but she isn't upset. Her eyes are moving slightly from side to side like she's reading a book. The cogs are turning.

'What is it?' I ask. She holds her hand up as if to say *I've got an idea but I don't know how good it is.*

'What if Rigel's right?' we're both confused. 'What if we could find out more information on the Beings that would have it out for him?' she's spirited as she speaks. 'What if we could find out where they are?'

'And how are we going to do that?' Rigel asks sceptically.

'By getting it from the Fleet's Database.' She replies with certainty.

She explains her idea of getting the information by using her access into the Fleet Sector and using the computers to find out what she needs over our stew. Given the time we decide to rest up and start fresh in the morning. The smell of the stew making my mouth water. Rigel could easily be a chef but he won't give up this life now. He says he's too use to it.

She holds me tight when we lie in bed that night, her head on my chest.

'How're you feeling?' I ask knowing the state she was in earlier.

'I'm alright.' She replies and I believe her. 'You and Rigel have given me a new hope.' I squeeze her tight for a moment. I love that I can help her that I can be there for her. I'm not sure how but, for her and in her words, I make her feel safe.

'It's a good plan.' I tell her in case she feels any doubt about it. She pulls herself back to lie her head on the pillow beside me. She stares intensely at me. This girl makes me feel like I'm needed just by giving me a look. She runs her hand through my hair before gently gliding her fingertips down my cheek.

'Thank you.' She says with full sincerity. 'For sticking by me. You could've easily left me there on that beach. I would've understood. But you helped me.'

Everything about this, looking at her lying next to me, is perfect. She's perfect. Flawed in ways but she's so perfect.

'I love you.' I tell her.

She doesn't say it back but she leans in and kisses me. i move closer to her, placing my hands on her waist. She runs her hand up my chest, sending me wild with this simple action. Moving my body on tops of her she wraps her leg around mine. Unlike before, this time I don't stop it.

Files

I make my way down the hall with my head held high and
shoulder back. I tried to make myself look presentable
albeit my lack of desire to do so. My hair down with the sides
twisted into a simple half up hairstyle. My plain ivory coloured
vest and navy skinny jeans made me feel like I was wearing
luminous yellow. Even though I was the only one who knew
why I was making my way down this hall, I felt like I might as
well have had a sign above my head saying I was going to
steal confidential information. I have every right to be there,
except I am a fraud. My cover story is going to be that I want
information about the investigation. To see how far they've
got this time.

My heart is in my mouth as the thumping deafens me. My
backpack hanging over one shoulder swings from side to side.
The guards at the door look surprised to see me. I ignore them,
purposely avoiding their gaze as I push the door open. I've
timed it right as the soldiers are just changing over from shifts.
I spy a free computer and make a beeline for it.

'Adelina?' I spin to see the person who had said my name.
Only my father calls me by my full name unless we're hosting.
Our guests then refer to me as Adelina. I smile as I see him. He
still looks tired. I don't think he's slept. Is he really suffering at the
loss of his grandchild? If he is then why hasn't he contacted

me in the last few weeks? Why hasn't he reached out? We could've supported each other.

'Dad.' I push my annoyance aside and smile at him hugging him tight. I've missed him.

'What are you doing here?' he asks in disbelief.

'I wanted to know if you'd gotten anywhere.' I half lied without missing a beat.

My father leads us to the side room where I was given Rigel's file a few weeks earlier having general chit chat about how we'd been. He takes the seat opposite me behind the desk.

'Did you get anywhere with that Noble?' I hesitate. Uh, yeah I did but I won't be telling you about it.

'He's stubborn. I'm still trying to get the information.' I lie. He's a bit stubborn, yes, but I have the information I need, not what they want.

My father goes to say something but a knock at the door stops him. He excuses himself and leaves the room. That was short and sweet. I eye the computer on the desk, I glance at the door checking no one is there and make my way round.

I type at the keys logging on, searching as fast as I can through the database. My eyes furiously scan over the screen for Rigel's file and the list of names he gave me. I type them out frantically, constantly checking the door. I click the files to print on each of the names. The printer stirs to life and the pages print quickly. I shove them into my back pack before they've even finished printing. I mutter under my breath for them to hurry up as I was getting impatient aware that my father could come back in at any moment. Luckily I manage to log off and sit back in my seat, pretending like I hadn't moved, just as the door reopens. My father pokes his head round the door and beckons me to come into the main room.

We walk together in comfortable silence towards the meeting table where Costello stands. He straightens up when he sees me. He doesn't hide his surprise.

'I wasn't expecting to see you here, Princess.'

'Well, I hadn't heard anything since your 'inspection' so I thought I'd come and find out for myself.' I say, trying to rub in the fact that he had run out of leads. I hope he feels the same annoyance I did when he told me they had no more evidence to follow. The look on his face and low growl under his breath lets me know I was successful. I don't usually set out to get petty revenge but I felt it was unacceptable.

My father, seemingly oblivious to my dig, offers me my usual seat. I take it and straight away it feels wrong. It doesn't feel like my seat any more but I remain anyway. I don't want to be here. I'm itching to get back to the cave. It feels more like a rogue rescue than a Fleet responsibility. I need to go. I'll only be holding back information. They wouldn't believe me anyway. Without any hard proof, Rigel would be arrested and charged with a crime he didn't commit.

My father and Costello take their usual seats, Costello opposite and my father at the head of the table. Something doesn't feel right though. I look round the meeting room.

'Where is everybody?' I asked getting nervous and purposely not tucking my chair in all the way.

'Out.' Costello replies bluntly.

'I can see that.' My reply just as blunt.

'They're out following a lead.' My father answers through supressed annoyance as if he's dealing with two squabbling siblings. I gave him an expectant look waiting for him to tell me what lead he was talking about.

'There's been a tip off about a sighting of Allard near the South Side of the Silver Forest.' I'm confused, how would anyone know he was in the Silver Forest? And why on the polar side of the forest which was miles off. I decide not to ask question even though loads were going through my mind like, who would see him out there?

'So what do you know for definite?' I ask. I don't really know why I want to know. They had nothing last time and everything I know is conflicting with their knowledge. I want to go. Even though I haven't known Jake a month yet and only met Rigel yesterday, I trust them more than I trust the Fleet now. I feel like they've at least tried to help despite having nothing.

Costello and my father exchange a look. The kind of look which said 'are you going to tell her or am I?' The kind of look that makes my stomach drop.

'What?' I ask my voice a smidge higher than I wanted it to be. That have a note difference in my pitch gave away my fear. Costello sits upright in his chair, letting me know he was going to be the one to do the talking.

'We have nothing left to go on. The case has gone cold.' His tone mono but his face look defeated. The glow in his eyes looked drab. 'If we don't find anything by the end of the week we'll have to close the case.'

'What?! No! You can't! Dad!' what in this world was I hearing? They're going to give up? No way!

'I'm sorry love.' My father tells me remorsefully.

'So that's it?! You're giving up? Are you for real?!' I yell more at Costello. 'She's is my daughter! If that isn't enough she's a Princess! I can't believe I ever trusted you!' I do believe I do. I trusted them to never give up on me or my daughter. As quickly as I got angry I calm myself and turn to my father my words like ice. 'I trusted you.' I turn my back on them both, done with the pair of them. I pace quickly out of the room ignoring my father's calls and apologies.

My footsteps echoing as I make my way back down the hall, it dawns on me. I no longer belong here. The Fleet isn't who I am anymore. Everything I believed during training and being recruited until this mission is wrong. I no longer believe in their ways. I know they've spent longer on cases with even less evidence and yet here they were considering closing the case on my child. I hate them.

I met Jake back at the craft. Everything I hope is now with him. The moment I see him my pace gets faster until I'm running to him and almost knock him over when I reach him and throw my arms around him hysterically explaining what I was just told. We make our way back to the cave as fast as possible. I give them the file unable to bring myself to look, instead I curl up on the chair, lost, ruminating Costello's words over and over again. Rigel reads over his file finally finding out the evidence that lead the Fleet to believe he was at fault. He throws the file in anger across the small room, frightening me from my daze.

'I can't ruddy believe it!' he yells 'that's all they had?! 'A ruddy black handkerchief and some black feathers.' Jake looks at me stunned.

'That's it? That's all they had on you?' he echoes in disbelief. 'What made them think that was you?'

'I haven't used black handkerchiefs in years and t' feathers are from t' local birds. It doesn't even say what kind of birds. Ruddy ridiculous. All it says is it 'shows similarities'! That's it!' I shake my head. They allowed me to believe it was definitely him. All they had was feathers because it's something that is identifiable to him.

'What were the other leads?' I turn to them both. 'They told me they were looking into other leads.' Jake picks up the strewn file and skims over the shuffled pieces of paper.

'Nothing.' He answers. 'There's nothing in here.' I held my hand out for the files and looked over them myself. I sat there making sure I read every word. In the mismatched pieces of paper I read over Rigel's criminal history, fact file with age, address etc. Details of his crimes and the evidence of the black items and the tests they carried out on them, but no results. Did they get results they weren't expecting? If I hadn't accessed them without permission I'd storm in there and demand answers. Frustrated I threw the file too, mimicking Rigel's actions, the anger bubbling within me.

I try to get into my Fleet soldier mind set. I try to analyse it in my head as they would've at the time. They would've walked in and made a note of the layout, broken objects, if the curtains were open or closed, if anything was obviously missing and take pictures of the room to coincide with their version. If they found items belonging to Rigel in the room then where was it? I promptly gather the papers again and search for the facts on the room. Upon finding it I let the others go and they float to my feet like snow. I examine the picture. The handkerchief is screwed up by the bed and the feathers in, an almost perfect line, by the window. It's obvious to me it was staged. I'm finding it harder and harder to think like them. To be objective like them. I'm not them! Knowing how they think though lets me though that without any evidence they would've had no choice but to pursue Rigel. One of the worst feelings in the world is knowing the truth and not being able to do anything about it.

I sigh and drop the picture to the floor. I hold my head in my hands, feeling unable to cope with the situation much more. I feel like my head will explode otherwise. I don't feel stable in my feet as I feel my knees begin to tremble. I feel so weak and drained from this whole thing. All I want is Lyra back. I collapse back down in the chair exhausted.

'Rigel...' I look up to see Jake with his hand out to Rigel with one of the files in his hand, his expression stern. Rigel takes the papers with apprehension. I wait the anticipation making me lean forward expecting some kind of breakthrough.

The colour drains from Rigel's face as he reads the file. He looks as though it was the last thing he wanted to find out.

'What is it?' I ask unable to stand waiting. I can't be patient any more.

'I know who has her.' Rigel says full of dread. The tone of his voice making me once again fearful. 'Rapha Blagden has escaped prison.'

The Next Step

The dull light of the Orb only enhanced the age on Rigel's face. He's not said much since he found out about Blagden's escape. I've never heard of him, he's never said anything about him. I feel a little betrayed that he's never spoke to me about it. The silence has been...annoying. What has this Rapha somebody done that's so bad that Rigel is afraid of?

'Rigel?' Lina speak finally breaking the tension. Gingerly he looks up at her. 'Who is Rapha Blagden?'

He lets out a sigh like he's been holding his breath, now ready to talk.

'Rapha is a Centrosapian.' Judging by the look Lina's face she hadn't heard of that either. Rigel described the species to us. Tall, usually large built creature, although he says that Rapha is unusually small build to their average measurements. His dark skin has a teal hue but protrudes black spikes in a Mohawk style from their head as well as from their cheekbones. They have sharp claws that can tear flesh with ease. Their dark pigment allowing them to hide well in the dark but it means they don't fare well in bright light. He recalls that unlike average Centrosapians', Blagden had rotted teeth and a tick that caused his head to tilt to the side involuntarily.

'But what did you do to make him an enemy?' Lina asks the question I was going to.

Rigel continues to explain how Rapha was selfish, disowned by his kind and left to find suitable shelter for his sun sensitive skin. He came across him one night attempting to break the security fence for the city's Food Storage Centre, where all the rations are kept and given out for everyone's fair share of work.

'I asked him just what he thought he was doing. I shone my torch on him and he retreated a bit before ignoring me to get through the fence again.' He tried to talk to him only to be met with hisses. He tripped the alarm in doing so which meant the security would soon be there. Rigel followed him he held him back from being caught by the spotlight above the centre.

'He was too weak to fight me off.' He confesses with a voice full of sadness. 'I wouldn't let him go until he told me what he was up to.'

Turns out he was going to break into the centre and steal as much food as he could for his lair. A new home since being cast out. It meant hundreds of hardworking residents would be without food for months while everyone worked to get back on track. Supplies were already low due to it being winter and the crops wouldn't grow as well due to the cold weather. He knew he had to stop him. Rapha's small frame meant he eventually wriggled free the second Rigel's grip loosened and headed to the Centre, immediately tearing into the side with his claws as if it was a knife in butter. Even though he was weak he was pretty fast, at that speed he could empty the Centre within minutes. The security was closing in by then, he could hear their shouts. Rapha started digging into the ground which revealed a tunnel for him to drop the food into. To stop him from getting away with so much food Rigel decided there was only one thing he could do to save, potentially, hundreds of people from starvation. He quickly looked around and found a thick branch thanks to the overhead spotlight still panning the area. He picked it up, raised it and struck the weak creature in the leg.

'It cracked. He was so weak his leg broke like a twig.' His tone full of remorse and regret.

'I scarpered and security found him. Turned out the lad was connected to other crimes throughout t' city. He was sent to prison and was flagged as a risk to the city. He was meant to serve 30 years...' he trailed off. 'I guess he never forgave me.'

'And now he's escaped.' I say to the floor. 'Is really twisted enough to kidnap a child to frame you?'

He says that Centrosapians' are kind natured creatures but Rapha is one of the exceptions and is one to hold the slightest of grudges.

'After that night I did my research. Found an elderly Bonytriggerdi who knew of the Centrosapians' and was able to tell me where to find them.' I see the memory flash across his eyes as he scratches his scar. 'I found his tribe. They said Rapha had been...different all his life. Causing trouble and lives to be at risk with no kind or concern for who got hurt. He was cast out for being a danger to his kind. I wouldn't put kidnap past him.'

'If he's escaped, how come no one knows about it?' I ask

'They won't.' pipes Lina. 'He's potentially very dangerous. If the Fleet believe he's that much of a threat they would keep it within the Fleet as not to cause wide spread panic.'

More deafening silence as we all contemplate the situation.

'What do we do now?' Lina breaks the silence. 'Do we find him?'

'We don't even know if he has her! Let alone where he is.' I exclaim trying to bring perspective. Her face falls and guilt eats away at me but I can't risk losing her to this unhinged Being on a limb. I reach my arm out to her.

'I might know where he is.' Rigel pipes up. 'I'll take you there. We'll go together.'

Lina's head pops up and a shine in her eyes lights up her face. I pull away from her – this is madness!

'Stop! Everybody stop!' silence. They stare at me like I have a second head. When did I become the responsible one? 'We can't just run to a place with no plan! If he's as dangerous as you say he is then he might just kill us all!'

'Not like you to think ahead, Jake.' Rigel says. He's right it's not. I usually just think of it and go head first. Lina is the one to be cautious. I've seen it in everything she does, from the way she welds to the way she moves, like she thinks it all through first. 'You're right though. We can't just rush there on a hope.' Finally, some sense. 'We'd need weapons. No telling what how he'd react.'

What! This can't be real.

'And where are we meant to get weapons from!' I declare. Am I the only sane one here!

'Leave it to me.' I turn to see Lina with the most determined look on her face. I could tell now there was going to be no talking her out of it. Her cautiousness gone. Taking a deep breath I decide to get on board. No use fighting it.

'Ok.' I say giving in.

Jake and I flew back to the city. Raced up the stairs back to our room, I need my Fleet ID. It was in my drawer. I need it to get what we need. This is no longer the Fleet's mission as far as I was concerned. This is now a vigilante case. If they were giving up I sure as anything wasn't. I ran so fast I didn't see anything or anyone in the reception or the hallways. I was focused on the ID.

I burst through the room, practically flew across the room to my drawer, only stopping once I found it. I pocketed it as I went to leave only to be met with Stevens and Costello with Jake by the scruff of his arms. Their expressions told me they weren't here for a nice catch up. My excitement evaporated.

'Where have you two been the last two days?!' Stevens shouted, pushing Jake into the room. 'Do you know how busy we've been?! It's been swamped down there and you've been off gallivanting?! You'd better have a good enough excuse! Start talking!'

I froze. I didn't know what to do. I locked eyes with Costello. What was he even doing here? With a slight tilt of the head he told me he wanted a word. Creeping past Stevens, who was now subjecting Jake to his wrath of anger, I walked towards the corner of the room Costello had indicated to.

'Do you want to tell me why you were really at the Meeting Hall yesterday?' he whispered sternly. I felt a heat prickle up my spine at the realisation that he might know what I'd done.

'I told you. I wanted to know what was going on with the case.' I replied trying to maintain my composure.

'I've spoken to Colonel Stevens.' He informs me as if to say he already knew what was going on so I shouldn't even bother lying. 'He came to me after not seeing you yesterday or today. He thought you might be somewhere injured. He wanted Search and Rescue to look for you. He wasn't pleased when I told him I'd seen you this morning. I know you haven't been here. Where have you been? What do you know?' his low voice steaming with demand.

'We had a day off if you must know.' It wasn't exactly lying but there was no way I was telling him the truth. 'We had a day out of the city.'

The Commander took a step closer to me, trying to intimidate me with his looming stature. Hasn't he got it by now? It won't work.

'If you know something to do with the case then you are obliged by oath to share with the Fleet.' It sounds like a threat. It's true I swore by oath when I became a member of the Fleet. But what good is it when I know they wouldn't listen to me? *Oh by the way, the suspect is hiding out in a cave and he isn't the suspect it's actually an escaped prisoner of a species you've never heard of so therefore you're going to think I made it up.*

'What I know,' I begin annoyed now. Stevens still shouting at Jake and Jake giving as good as he got. 'Is that you've given up on my daughter. I haven't.'

I go to take my share of the shouting from the Colonel when he speaks again.

'I think from now on you should leave the investigating to me.' As if!

'Like I'm going to allow you to do that.' I retort.

'If you're withholding information then I'm going to have no choice but to withdraw your involvement form the case.' I've never known a Being irritate me as much as him.

'Go ahead.' He looks surprised.

He wasn't expecting that and takes a second to make a comeback.

'While you are on my Fleet,' He sounds a little flustered, trying to regain control, 'you are my responsibility-'

'So was your last Second.' He shuts up. I shouldn't have said that. That wasn't his fault. That was an accident and everyone knew it. Without saying another word he makes his way over to Stevens who was *still* shouting. I begin to feel the guilt once again eat away at me but as my eyes fall to the floor I notice something.

His ID clasp on his belt was open.

Glancing up quick I saw he was now getting at Jake too. Carefully, without even thinking, I brought up my right hand, the one that wouldn't be in the corner of his eye. With my index finger I lifted up the open clasp and used my middle finger and thumb I lifted the card with great care and swiftness as

I could manage. Any vibration felt by Costello would get me in huge trouble.

Quick as a flash I pocket the card just moments before Stevens turns his wrath to me.

He's quite scary when angry. I much prefer his happy-go-lucky presence. He shouts at me but I have no time for this. I have other places to be. I'll deal with all this later.

'Enough!' I shout stunning them all. Short little me, standing up to two broad figures towering over me. 'If you must know, bunking off was my idea. It was wrong and I apologise and I'll make up for it later.' They just stand there silent. 'Now if you'll excuse me.' Without giving them a chance to answer I beckon Jake to follow me which he does like a dog squeezing by the two men like an animal between fence panels.

My short legs stride along the corridor with such determination that Jake has to almost run to keep up with me.

'That was great!' he grins when he catches up with me. I grin back taking his hand and we hurry down the corridor.

I left Jake in the reception of the Mechanics Sector to prepare the air craft while I rushed off to the Fleet's HQ.

If my watch is right the guard outside the meeting hall should be changing over, giving me 5 minutes to get in and get out with weapons I need before the new guards arrive to begin their shift.

My timing is perfect I get there just as the klaxon sounds. I peak round the corner, making sure I keep out of sight, to see the guards step down and leave their positions. The moment they're out of sight I race to the door, heaving it open. As I thought the room is empty. Everyone out on training or investigating whatever they'd been assigned to now. I run to the weapons room as fast as I can, my backpack, currently empty, swinging freely on my back.

Costello's ID card ready in hand I scan the card before pressing in the code with my knuckle. The door unlocks, every second feeling lengthy. I check my watch 4 minutes. I run down the room grabbing Nysa guns, a couple of spare Cariopius and a net gun, a specially made gun that shoots a net which tightens up once it hits its target. My bag now full I race, now weighed down a bit, towards the door. Closing it behind me so it locked. I rub the ID car over my top to rid it of prints and drop it in the room. Hopefully Costello will think it just fell out of his holder.

Run. I run to the door, heaving it open once more and running down the hall to my previous hiding place where I stop. I listen. I hear the door clasp shut and I let out a breath like I'd been holding it in the whole time. I check the time, 30 seconds left. Luckily I got out in time as I hear the footsteps of the next guards coming down the hall. Relived I continue down the hall back to Jake waiting for me in the craft.

Rapha Blagden

I force the controls forward to speed through the air, I want to get there as soon as possible. It's been a weird few days and I want some kind of normality. I want Lina in my life still. Will I still see her once she goes back to being part of the Fleet? I don't really want to know but at the same time I do so I can move on.

We get forced back in our seat as the power of the craft lurches forward with power. Cloud, orange from the light of the sun, seem to make a path before us in the bright clear blue sky ahead. I glance at her sat next to me. She's in her own world, staring out the window but not fixed on the view of trees below.

'What's wrong?' I ask placing my hand on her thigh. She breaks from her thoughts, letting out a tired sigh.

'I don't know who I am anymore.' She says.

'What do you mean?'

'I feel like I'm starting to unravel.' I try my best to look at her in between keeping my eyes on the sky ahead. 'Two days in a row I've broke the law by stealing files I didn't have permission to and I've just stolen a load of weapons using someone else's ID. I don't know who I am anymore.'

'You had someone else's ID?' this was news to me. She nods.

'I took Costello's ID when he wasn't looking. I used it to gain access to the weapons.' She puts her head in her hands in frustration.

'It's ok.' I try to comfort her while keeping control of the craft.

'Is it?' she asks with an almost sarcastic tone. 'I've done things I never thought I would and now I'm risking everything and could get you and Rigel in trouble!'

'For Lyra.' I say simply putting an end to her conflict. I see it in her face. All her guilt fading away.

'You're a mother.' I state. 'You'll do anything for your child. Rigel and I know what we're getting into. If we get in trouble, we'll deal with it.' I glance at her again. 'Ok?'

'Ok.' She replies quietly. We fly in silence for a short while before she speaks again.

'I'm going to leave the Fleet.'

'What? Why?'

'I realised I'm not like them.' I'm going to get whiplash if I keep trying to look at her and fly so I decide its best just to look ahead.

'Everything I thought I knew about being a part of the Fleet is wrong. I'm not one of them anymore.' She pauses. 'When we find Lyra I'm leaving the Fleet.'

I say nothing. My heart feels like it's fallen out of my chest. She's leaving the Fleet. She won't be my Spare anymore. She'll move back to the castle. I'll never see her again. I was kidding myself, believing I could be with a Princess. I run my hand over my forehead, brushing back a lock of hair from my eye.

Without really paying much attention I ease up on the controls and slowing the craft down as I grieved for a love I haven't even lost yet.

'Are you ok?' she asks. I remain silent, keeping my thoughts to myself. I daren't tell her how I'm feeling. She said herself she didn't know if her feelings were real. Now I'm certain I was just a shoulder to cry on. Yet I want to tell her exactly what I'm thinking. I want to argue with her. If I argue with her then maybe it won't hurt as much when she's gone. I want to ask her about us, if there will ever be an us, which is seeming less and less likely, but how do I ask?

'Have I upset you?'

'You know how I feel about you!' I snap feeling my anger rise. 'When you get Lyra what happens to us? Are you going back to your castle and forget about me?! You know what?! I don't even want to know!' I crack before she can answer.

'I'd still want to see you.' She mutters after a moment. 'I might not know my feelings for definite but I hope they're real. I'd want to at least give us a go.'

My annoyance quickly melts away at this admission. Boy do I feel stupid. Why did I get angry? I could've just asked her. You idiot, Jake.

'I'm sorry.' I say.

'I'm sorry too.' She says.

'Why are you sorry?'

'I must have made you feel like I was using you.' She look delicate again. 'That was never the intention.'

Taking one hand off the controls I clasp her hand in mine to tell her I forgave her. I knew she was just trying to find her daughter.

'Let's not talk about this anymore.' I smile at her. 'Let's go find Lyra.'

Her face immediately has a grin spread across her face and she leans over and give me a quick hug and I prepare to land to pick up Rigel. I can't stay angry at her. She was just desperate.

Reaching out, she runs her fingers lightly through my brown hair. Lifting my hand up to her I pull her hand to my lips and kiss it.

But what if we do give it a proper go? What if it becomes really serious and she wants me to meet Lyra as her boyfriend? What if it gets to the point of marriage? Can I really be a father, even a step father?

I push the thoughts out of my mind to deal with at a later date. Now wasn't the time to be afraid.

We race east across the sky, with Rigel sat in the back, towards the Food Storage Centre. Soaring high over the surrounding woodland before large farming fields pan out beneath us. Endless rows of crops that haven't sprouted yet, probably because it could be one of the fields that has just been harvested and replanted for the next season. Each crop has 4 fields so one field can be harvested once every three months. It's been like that for about 10 years to keep up with the population. Jake and Rigel chat away about something or other, I'm not really listening to be honest. All my senses have been heightened looking out for the Centre, glancing left, right and every direction in between.

We fly over more fields before it comes into sight dead ahead.

'There it is!' I shouting, breaking them from their conversation about who cares what and pointing in its direction. Jake adjusts the steering controls so we head directly towards it. My heart is hammering against my chest as the desire I didn't expect to feel burns inside in my want to be there like a child excited about a day out.

'Best land 'bout 'ere.' Rigel instructs Jake. About a quarter of a mile away from the Centre. Jake has the hang of the craft now and takes it down, seeks out a clear landing spot at the edge of the fields and lands in almost one smooth movement.

The legs of the craft touch the ground with a slight bump as the suspension continues move before stopping post landing.

We clamber out of the craft. I swing the backpack onto my shoulder and look in all directions trying to get my bearings from us to the Centre. I feel a hand slide along my lower back. I turn and make eye contact with some blue eyes that make my stomach flip. I feel a smile cross my face. I lean into him and his arm stretches round me bringing me into a hug.

'I'm scared.' I whisper into his shoulder. Taking the backpack from me he slips his hand into mine and we all walk towards the centre in silence. I think the reality has hit home. We don't know what we're going to find, if we find anything. What is the plan if we find Rapha? Do we just aim our weapons at him threatening to fire until he talks?

We walk over a more rocky terrain compared to the fields and the landing spot. We wobble at time as we almost lose our balance. The September sun beats down on us, making me feel sleepy, the Centre slowly growing in size as we get closer. Rigel decides to put himself in charge as he discusses what he believes is the best course of action when we get there. We don't dispute it. He's had experience with Rapha, although brief, he knows he's unhinged. He's seen just how fast his species is. He has seen first hands just how sharp his claws are. If they can tear through metal like he described in his story, I hate to think what damage they could do to flesh.

He decides it's best to start by finding the tunnel he'd made, hopefully it won't have been filled. He will lead the way. He will keep a look out as he knows what to look for. If need be he will talk to Rapha.

'And if he attacks?' Jake asks. Rigel's face looks grave.

'Then I will fire.' He says sternly. 'I've been inside before. You kids are young with a life ahead a ya. Don't throw it away.'

He was willing to take the blame for something that involved all three of us? I don't think so. If he has to pay the price, we all will. He knows that. I hope he does.

The air feels dry when I breathe in. each step builds up more and more anxiety in my chest. I want to run and get away from this all but I know I can't. My eyes feel like they're burning. Jake tugs my arm and I look up from watching each steps over the rocks underfoot on this dry terrain. I can see by his eyes that he's worried about me. I'm so grateful to him. And Rigel, of course. But Jake, I haven't asked him to help me, I didn't even expect him to forgive me for lying to him. He just picked me up and said 'let's go'. I know I will never find a man like him. I will never be able to thank him for his help. I know I want to give us a go after all of this but I know I'll never let him go. I hope it works between us.

20 minutes since we landed we arrived at the Centre. It felt like hours. A tall rectangular cream coloured building, faded and dirty from time, lay behind a chain linked fence. The fence only put there to line the edge of the site.

'Over here.' Rigel calls pointing out a large cut hole in the fence, the edges of the cut links worn soft over time. The fence was cut some time ago.

'Looks like they never fixed It.' he states, more an out loud thought that a comment to either Jake or I. I brush loose hair out of my face, scraping it behind me ear.

'Are we just going to look at it?' I say, my patience wearing thin at the thought of being within reach of Lyra. It's been the best part of a month since she was taken. Rigel steps through the opening ducking under the top if it briefly catching his beaten old jacket on the now blunt spikes of the fence. We follow after as he goes directly to where the tunnel opening would've been.

Jake and I struggle to keep up with Rigel as he speed walks toward his destination. He's a man on a mission. He knows where he's heading and no one is stopping him. Not that we plan to stop him. He's far ahead of us when he suddenly stops. We don't see why until we reach him.

In front of him lies and old dirt pile, judging by the colour of the dirt it's been there a while. I'm confused for a moment. I look at Rigel's face to see an expression of disbelief. Quickly I look up and see just how close we are to the Storage Centre. It towers over all three of us as my world crashes down around as the truth dawns on me. This was meant to be the opening to the tunnel! But its filled in. everything around me blurs and my thudding heartbeat pretty much blocks all other sounds in my ears. I struggle for breath, feeling knees thud into the hard, dusty ground.

'What are we going to do now?' I whisper to myself full of self-pity and panic at the thought of never seeing my daughter again.

After all this. Where do we go from here? I look to Rigel for an answer but he looks as though he's just had his world turned upside down whereas Lina, crumpled on the floor looks as though hers has collapsed.

Quickly I look around as though the answer will just be lying on the ground. The ground? That's it! Tunnels as underground! What if they only filled in the entrance?!

'Would they have filled in the tunnel or just the opening?' I ask myself. Rigel's attention turns to me at this question. I turn to the path we just took. Rigel watches me like he's observing an animal and trying to figure out my next move. Which way would the tunnel go through? It could snake anywhere underneath us. The only way to know that is by the entrance which, of course, is filled in. I can almost feel my brain coming to life as it furiously searches for a way around the problem.

I turn my attention back to the small mountain of dry soil that marked the entrance. The only way to find out the direction of the tunnel is through there but there's too much dirt to move.

In my mind block I allow the backpack to fall to my feet. The backpack! I forgot I had it. Within seconds I fished out one of the Nysa guns Lina packed. If the plan that's forming in my mind pans out as I think it will then I'll need the Nysa.

'Lina?' I get her attention. 'What do the pellets of this Nysa gun do?'

'Those ones are full of Petrolla Larvae.' She answers lifelessly. Brilliant, just what I need. the Larvae from the Petrolla bug, a vicious little creatin with multiple sharp teeth lining the whole of its mouth and dark grey webbed skin to fly easily from tree to tree, is like a strong acid like liquid. Strong enough to melt metal beams and severely burn flesh of any creature. It's a defence mechanism used by the bug. It would also make light work of the ground.

'Move her.' I order Rigel, aiming the gun to the ground at the side of the dirt hill. Rigel wastes no time in move Lina as he realises what it is I'm about to do. He gathers her off the ground and runs as fast as he can out of the firing zone.

The second they're safe enough I fire without hesitation. A rather muffled bang releases multiple pellets of the larvae into the ground melting it like hot water on ice until the larvae naturally, making a sizzling sound before it extinguishes itself once its spread out as far as it can.

At me feet a large hole forms revealing what I'd hoped. They only filled in the entrance, the rest of the tunnel was still there.

I'm feeling rather smug with myself and I can't hide it with a foolish smirk on my face. I tilt my head to see Lina and her face says it all. As Rigel lets out a loud and boisterous laugh her hope reignited, her eyes shining. She locks eyes with me and I can see just by the look on her face how grateful she is. She doesn't need to but she mouths the words *thank you* to me. She evens runs round the edge of the hole and flings her arms around me, nearly knocking me over, holding on to me like she'd never let go. She whispered the words *thank you* in my ear over and over again. She didn't need to thank me but it did make me feel appreciated and needed.

We didn't waste much time climbing down the hole, careful to avoid the left over larvae – that could still burn. Shaking a small Bio Orb, I pocketed this morning, the tunnel came to light and the direction of the tunnel spread out back in the direction we came in before bending to the left. The tunnel became lighter and I looked to see Lina clasping some kind of tool with a Bio Orb on to the belt loop of her trousers.

'What's that?' I asked upon clocking it.

'It a Cariopius.' She explained what it was as we walked down the tunnel. With my spare hand I handed out the other Nysas' so we were all protected. It sounds like a handy gadget. 'It even has a voice recorder and a tracking device. I've never used either though.' my ears prick at the mention of a tracking device. Images of her having it on while we were in the cave flashed through my mind.

Thankfully she finished with the revelation that she never used it so my worries evaporate as quickly as the formed.

We spend the rest of the journey in silence. I listen hard for any noise that could show let us know if Rapha was here. I lose track of time while in there, the darkness making me feel a little disorientated. I secretly fear that, as Rapha is a creature that hides well in the dark that he could be right behind us and we wouldn't even know.

We must have been walking 10 minutes, it could've been more, and I don't know when a dull light appears up ahead around the next left hand bend. I don't know how many bends we passed on the way here but now we know we'd found something. It could be anyone. All we could see from here was a flickering light.

I place my finger on the trigger and take a step in front of Lina. I don't care what happens to me but if he has Lyra then she needs to be ok for her. If she can get her and get away then everything will be fine, no matter what happens to me and Rigel. It'd be two against one but his abilities put him at an advantage to us. I take a step forward but Rigel stops me.

'I'll go.' He says setting his gun to fire. He strides forward and, despite his large frame, he doesn't make a sound. I hold my breath as I watch my dad walk towards the light into the room, terrified it might be the last time I ever see him. I take small steps behind him so Lina doesn't know how afraid I am. I want to be strong for her.

Rigel stops at the doorway, casting a huge shadow over the wall of the tunnel. His face lights up in wonder as his eyes scan over the room. His amazement vanishes as he squints, focusing on one point. He beckons us to him with an eager motion of his hand like he has something important to show us. The pair of us practically run to his side. We're both blown away by the cave we entered. The room lit up completely by one small Bio Orb, orange by the lack of natural light. The walls of the cave are covered in twinkling diamonds and other gems reflecting all the light so the cave is fully lit. If it wasn't for the enormity of the situation it'd be beautiful. I can't admire it too long though as Rigel points out to me a large round, honey coloured orb attached to what looked like some kind of root sprouting form the group. It doesn't take me long to see what Rigel sees.

I grab Lina by the arm distracting her from the beauty of the room. She needs to see this.

The hold the diamond encrusted cave had on me was broken by someone roughly grabbing my arm. I follow the arm to see Jake has a hold of me. I'm about to tell him off when I see that both he and Rigel are locked to one spot. Taking a step closer I try to see what has left them speechless.

Stepping in front of Jake so I could see. I see more diamonds lining the wall, the ground with different levels making natural steps further down the cave and large, smooth rounded curves of the walls. A large golden orb rooted in the ground, surrounded by a few smaller golden orbs. The larger one seems to have some sort of life form growing within it. A small humanoid in the fetal position. It makes me think of Lyra, she sleeps like that. On her side with her knees to her chest, one arm up by her head. The life form even looks as though it has two long braids going down its back.

125

A small smile to myself quickly wipes from my face as my stomach falls away from me. That isn't a life form growing in that giant spheroid-it's Lyra!

'LYRA!' I scream, running faster than I ever have in my life towards the sphere. I fall down one step, jumping back to my feet before any pain can be felt. I jump down the steps and fall to my knees when I reach her.

'Lyra...' I say to her, tears of relief streaming. I've found her!

'How do we get her out?' I ask panicking as Jake and Rigel catch up to me. 'Do we cut the root?'

It seemed plausible. The root was the only thing connected to the sphere. If we cut it then we could get her out. I draw the cutlass on my Cariopius. I raise it high ready to strike the roof. I prepared myself to put force behind the swipe. I move my arm down-

'I wouldn't do that if I were you.' A low, evil sounding voice says, making us all jump back.

'Who's there?! Who said that?!' demanded Jake as he and Rigel naturally position their selves around me and Lyra, instinctively ready to protect.

A dark blur moves from behind a curve in the cave wall behind us. It moves so fast I can only make out its dark blue colouring. Terror floods through me as I become aware that it can only be one Being.

Rapha Blagden.

He stops on top of the natural stairs which we were standing upon just a minute earlier.

Rigel description of him wasn't very scary, but now I'm horror struck. His tall, slim figure gave the illusion of a giant, his neck ticks present straightaway. One of the rows of black spikes on his left cheek were damaged, some even missing. The spikes on his other cheek and on his head still very much intact. He bares his rotted black teeth in a cruel, menacing grin.

Fight for Lyra

'Alright Rapha.' Rigel addresses him. Rapha's grin fades and he steps forward, limping on his right leg. Rigel's eyes falter in his lock with Rapha as he notices his leg. I realise that must have been the leg he broke all those years ago.

'Rigel.' Rapha greets him, his tone full of hate. 'It's been... how many years?'

'Twenty.' Rigel answers bluntly, his face contorted into a scowl.

'I spent a long time inside because of you.' Rapha limps down a steps talking as if the rest of us aren't here.

'See this?' he taunts, raising his right hand. The fingers and claws on one of his hands are broken and point in directions they shouldn't. 'This happened in my first week inside. Word got out about what I tried to do. The inmates were angry, said I could've harmed their families. They also did this to my face.' He points out his damaged spikes, his tone lacking remorse.

He lets out what can only be described as a hiss, full of anger and hatred. His next words seem to linger long after he spoke.

'They soon left me alone when I used my good hand to fight back.' He grinned with pleasure at the, no doubt, disturbing memory. 'I stuck them in one inmate's stomach. Ripped it open in one swift move. He guts fell out.' he laughed. One of those laughs that make your skin crawl. 'They would clear the halls for me after that.' He taunted relishing in the moment of making us recoil in shock. Rigel was right. He is unhinged. I've had enough already.

'We didn't come here for a catch up!' I snap. 'Let her go!' I demand pointing to Lyra in the sphere where Lina sat, arms over her with maternal instinct to protect her.

If he didn't like me butting in on his gloating, he didn't show it. Instead he folded his arms behind his back, straightening himself up. He currently has the upper hand and he knows it.

'I wouldn't cut that root if I were you.' He echoes himself, words sliding of his tongue and hanging in the air. He ignores me and addresses Lina. I don't want him anywhere near her or Lyra.

It annoys me. I just want to shoot him and go now. Just his presence is enough to irritate me.

'Cut that root,' he talks casually to Lina, limping towards her. 'And she'll be sucked into the ground. Never to be seen again.' He lets out a laugh from the belly. His twisted sense of humour means he's the only one who laughs.

Anger boils inside me so I take a step in front of Lina. I don't want him taking another step towards either of them.

'What's this? Trying to be the hero.' He mocks me. He'll never know the love I have for Lina, nor will he ever be the recipient of such love.

'What is it? How do we get her out?' Lina pleads with him, desperate to be with her little girl again.

'That.' He nods towards the cocoon with Lyra in. 'that is a Somnocomb. A pod in which whatever is inside, sleeps until it's released.' He pauses while his tick plays out.

'As for getting her out?' he smirks. 'If I told you that, you'd have her out of there and be out of here within a minute...and you've only just got here.' I can't believe this guy. That statement made me feel as though everything good in me just melted away. I can't bear to face Lina. I don't think I can bear the hurt in her eyes. I feel nothing but hate for him. Rigel might have pitied the poor, weak creature who was a little hungry but not me.

'Let her go!' I demand, holding my gun up to his, aiming at his face. He doesn't even flinch. I can't kill him. If I do that, we might never get Lyra out.

A Somnocomb? The substance within causes Hypersomnia. If he took her when she as asleep and was put in this sphere... then she's been asleep this whole time. She won't remember anything! She shouldn't have any traumatic memories from this. Can't say the same for me. Why has this obviously disturbed Being with a history of severely harming others, looked after my daughter? Well, in a way he's looked after her? Whatever the reason I don't care. She hasn't been hurt. That's all I care about. The solace I get from that fact rushes through me and all my worry and pain from the best part of the last month rushes over me. I'm no longer afraid. In its place is anger. Hatred. Loathing. All replace my fear.

I rise from my safe spot by Lyra. My jaw set, my expression serious. I step out from behind Jake, who tries to stop me by getting hold of my arm but I shake him off and aim my sight to Rapha. I look up at him from a few steps below him.

'I'm going to give you a choice, Rapha.' He scowls down at me. 'You either tell us how to get her out. We'll leave you in peace if you do.'

'What?!' Jake protests but I ignore him. I pause, waiting for a reaction but he continues to scowl.

'Or we'll catch you and send you back to prison where you belong.' I hold his gaze. I'm serious here. I won't go back on this. I'm not naïve though, I doubt he'll accept being given a choice like this. I'm not surprised when he give another belly laugh, he stops when he sees I haven't altered.

'There's one other option you haven't given me.' He says callously.

'What's that?' I ask. I don't care for his answer. I'm just humouring him.

'Death.' His answer makes my blood run cold. I can't let him die, he knows how to open the Somnocomb. He goes for me and I then flinch. I hear a gun fire and a flash of red Petrolla Larvae flash by my line of site so I draw my arms up over my head.

Only after the sizzle of the larvae fades out do I lower my arms. A large crevice in the side of the cave step has formed. My heart palpitating. That was terrifying. A familiar hand appears around my waist. Jake pulls me back behind him and we all intuitively form a protective circle, precariously searching for Rapha who has seemingly disappeared.

In my newly ignited fear I decide it's time to turn on the tracker of my Cariopius and wish for the Fleet to find us. Soon.

A blur passes up the wall by Rigel. He shoots. Misses creating another crevice in the rock wall.

His blurry silhouette then rushes past Jake who fires again. This happens a couple of times and each time he's too fast for us to hit, leaving multiple holes in the wall.

'Bloody hell!' Jake exclaims. 'You may have broken his leg but he still bloody moves fast!'

'STOP!' Rigel yells. 'If we keep shooting like this, t' cave will collapse!' I looked round at the cave now resembling some Swiss cheese. It's true, the structure of the cave could be compromised if we keep firing at an impossible target. Laughter echoes around us. I step back trying to protect the pod containing my precious child, unable to detect where the laugh is coming from.

'You get it now Allard.' Rapha gloats as he crawls out from his hiding place.

'This is my revenge for all those years ago.' He sneers. 'You should've just let me get on with my plan.'

'You've really held a grudge for all these years? You could've killed people!' Rigel's patience is now wearing thin. 'You were going to make people starve to death! Because you were selfish! I couldn't let you get away with that.'

Any sympathy Rigel had for the poor, weak Rapha he'd come across all those year ago was gone.

'I had plenty of time to think inside.' Rapha slunk closer, keeping enough distance to escape again. 'You see. They kept me in quarantine for a lot of the time.' His drawn out articulated words were oddly infuriating. 'I had a lot of time to think of how I was going to get you back.' He rushed, this time at a slower speed so he face Rigel head on. I tightened my finger around the trigger of my weapon, prepared to shoot.

'Of course I would love to kill you. I thought of how I'd do it too.' I see the colour drain from his weathered face. 'I'd cut you with the claws on my good hand. I'd leave long scars down your arms.' He talks as though he's had a casual run in with a friend at the shops. I feel myself begin to shake. I don't understand how someone could have a darkness like this inside of them.

'But why cut it short when I can watch you rot behind bars like I did?' he finishes. I can't even begin to understand his point of view in this.

'Is this for real?!' I'm meant to say in my head but no going back now. '*You* made that decision! *You* made the choice and *you* tried to follow it through! Yet you blame others!'

'It's his fault I got stopped!' Rapha snapped at me.

'He stopped you from hurting hundreds of people. All of this is *your* fault! No one else's!'

He doesn't like this. I pointed out his actions, made him accountable but in his head he's the victim. He lets me know this by letting out a roar that goes through me like nails on a blackboard. He attacks again. The shooting re-starts and I try to dodge the blue blur.

'Aargh!' I exclaim as a pain goes through my right arm. Looking down a see three or four thin lines of blood streaming down my arm. Jake pulls me between him and Rigel. Rigel clamps his hanker chief down on my arm to stem the bleeding tying it up with the corners as Jake continues to shoot. This time the shooting makes the ground beneath us tremble to the point pebbles begin to bounce on the rocks.

Rapha stops as Jake's gun runs out of the lava larvae, leaving him vulnerable to attack. Realising this, a vicious grin spread wide across his face from ear to ear.

All my senses stand to attention as the scene, to me, plays out in slow motion.

Fear comes over Jake's face as his life flashes before his eyes knowing that he could be dad within the next few seconds. My breath catches in my chest in fear of him dying. The positivity of finding the love of my life, Lyra, mixed with the negativity of losing the kindest man in my life being too punishing for me to contemplate.

Rapha makes his stance before running full speed towards Jake, good hand outstretched, claws poised. On autopilot I raise my gun, aiming just a little in front of his running direction and fire. BANG! A bright red flash and the blue blur get knocked sideways.

I hit him. My breath returns and I feel like I've been under water and I feel like my stomach has fallen away. I hit him. I saved Jake! Jake's face says it all. Shock. Relief. A shift in perspective. He runs to me, scoops me up and hold me in a way he hasn't before. He's upset but relieved. So am I. I ignore the pain and fresh warmth of the blood coming from my arm. His body – alive – being more important than my wound. We cry together and another pair of arms wrap around us sharing in our joy. We break away as an excruciating scream echoes through the cave. We look to where Rapha landed. He's alive. I hit him but I still missed. I only hit his head. His Mohawk is missing with remnants of singed black where it once was and some of his navy blue blood streaked down his sinister face.

Once again, infuriated he lets out his painful roar at us and goes to attack again. Only this time, he can't get the balance. He runs towards us but swerves from side to side with no control. It's as if the damage to his Mohawk has caused him to lose balance so he can't move in a blur anymore.

A flicker out the corner of my eye distracts me. Rigel has raised his gun to Rapha. For the first time, I see dread appear in his dark eyes. All this time his agility to move fast has given him the upper hand, now I've taken it away, he's just a lowlife, pathetic excuse of a creature. A mess of an existence with no concern for anyone but himself.

'You tried to hurt m' boy.' Rigel snarled. I've never seen him this angry before. 'You hurt this young woman. You kidnapped her little girl. And you tried to frame me. Give me one good reason not to kill you now.'

He holds his Nysa up to Rapha with a look in his eyes of pure hatred. If he kills him he'll be locked up.

'Don't!' I interrupt going to his side. 'You do this you will give him exactly what he wants. You'll be in prison for the rest of your life.' I try to reason with him. 'He gets away with it all.'

'Go on, Allard. I've caused so much hurt.' Blagden taunts. 'I deserve to die. Nothing will make you feel better than putting an end to me.'

'Don't listen to him!' I plead with my dad whose gaze was fixated on his aim.

'You said it yourself.' Rapha draws, head twitching again. 'I tried to kill your son. Get your revenge. Kill me.'

'No!' I stand in front of Rigel, blocking his line of sight to the gun. 'If you do this. *You* go to prison. Not him. *You.* What will we do if you're stuck inside? Who will I have? You're the only family I have.'

I see him falter. His scared eye twitches. My words sinking in. it pains him to give in but he does anyway. He throws his free arm around me and I hug back.

'Sorry lad.'

'You'll regret that.' Rapha seethes getting to his feet. He stumbles holding his head, obviously still in excruciating pain. His newly lost balance and swiftness making it difficult for him to remain upright. He staggers forwards claws out and poised trying to run towards the pair of them. The gun in Rigel's hand raises again, ready to shoot. I see Rigel's finger twitch to pull the trigger-

'They're in here!' a voice bellows in the direction of the tunnel we came through. We freeze stunned. Rigel lowers his gun post-haste as soldiers burst through into the cave. I check Lina to see she has a relieved look on her face as she still applies pressure to her arm. I have a gut feeling. I speed walk to her side as more and more voices come from the tunnel and more soldiers fill the cave.

'Did you have some to do with this?' I ask in lowered tone.

'Yes.' She admits guiltily holding up her Cariopius. Of course! The tracker. 'I was scared. I didn't know what else to do. I panicked!' she tries to justify her actions but I don't care. I silence her by putting my arms around her minding her injured arm.

'Miss Lune.' The stern voice of Commander Costello addresses her. 'A word.'

She breaks away from me. I turn my attention to Rapha who's fighting being arrested. A soldier comes from my side and tries to cuff me.

'What're you doing?!' I protest.

Rigel who's being cuffed. He doesn't fight though.

'STOP!' the room falls into eerie silence at the demand of Lina, although short in stature, standing tall and fierce against a whole army who stood to her attention.

'Let these two go.' She ordered. The arresting soldiers looked at each other as though to mentally ask each other who they listen to, their Princess or their Commander.

'Do no such thing!' Costello orders.

'They're innocent.' Lina stands up to Costello. 'All of this is because of me.' It made compelling watching seeing short Lina stand up against a towering figure like Costello who both out ranked each other in their own ways.

'Even if I'm expected to believe that they're suspects and will be held until our investigation is complete.' He tells her. 'Take them away!'

'NO! Take them over there!' she orders the soldiers by pointing to the other side of the cave without breaking her death glare at Costello. If looks could kill, he'd be 6 foot under by now. The soldiers, unsure of whose orders to follow, drag us to the other side of the cave as Rapha is dragged away through the tunnel.

'Don't you punish them for my decisions!' I scold Costello as a medic comes to quickly bandage my arm just well enough until we got back to the city.

'You're *decisions* will be held accountable for, don't worry about that.' He seethes.

'All of this was me!' I try to explain. 'I withheld information from the Fleet. I stole the files. I stole the weapons-'

'By listing my ID card.' He interrupts.

'Yes.' I confess.

'You purposely withheld information,' he growls at me, 'when you were obligated by oath to share-'

'Would you have really believed me?!' this shuts him up. 'If I had come into the meeting room telling you I'd found Rigel and he was innocent? No you would've found him, arrested him and probably charged him with a crime he didn't commit!'

We both pause for a second, both angry with the other. Both knowing we did wrong.

'I know I did wrong and will accept any punishment that is deemed fit. I withheld valuable information, I stole confidential files and I took weapons without consent. All that I hold my hands up to...but look...'

I lead him to the Somnocomb. His hardened expression softens when he sees who is lying within it.

'Oh my...she's here.' he's speechless.

'We don't know how to get her out.' I stress. 'Blagden wouldn't tell us how.'

Costello crouches down to the pod. He places his hand over it.

'So it wasn't Rigel?' he sounds remorseful.

'No.' I concur. 'Did you know about Rapha?'

'It was one of my first cases when I got promoted to Second.' He confides. 'We had an alert to a break in at the Food Storage Centre. When we arrived, we saw someone run away, leaving behind this undernourished, unusual creature with one leg bent the wrong way.' He pauses at the memory.

'He was vicious, cut some of the soldiers who tried to restrain him. We actually found this cave.' He looks around the crater filled cave. 'We thought filling in the entrance would be the end of it.'

He turns back to the pod. 'I haven't seen one of these in years.'

'You've seen a Somnocomb before?!' my attention peaking. 'Do you know how to get her out?!'

He runs his hand down to the twisted end. He simply pulls some of the spiked ends and the pod comes to life. The thought of the pod retreating into the ground as Rapha had said it would if we cut to roof. To my amazement it scrunches up even more before unwinding itself and releasing the gloop inside onto the floor, Lyra gliding out across the ground like my socks on the polished floors of the castle.

I rush to her stopping place and scoop her up in my arms letting out happy sobs as I hold her close.

I wipe of the rest of the gloop that covers her, which is surprisingly easy to do, and she stirs.

'Morning Mummy.' She say sleepily snuggling into me and wrapping her little arms around me.

'Hello darling.' I tell her, holding onto her like I'm never going to let go.

'Why are you crying, Mummy?' she asks confused and obviously unaware of the last months goings on.

'I'm fine, darling. Honest.' I promise her, holding her close again.

Home

I cling to my pyjama clad child like glue. There was no way I was letting her go now.

We climb up to the surface to be greeted with one of the Fleet's largest aircrafts already stowing Jake's craft into it.

'What will happen now?' I ask Costello as we slowly make our way to the craft.

'We'll need evidence from all three of you.' He tells me honestly. 'The worst Rigel and the boy will get is probably a warning or fine for handling stolen weaponry. You, on the other hand, you broke more serious laws and will most likely get a sentence of some sort.'

'I'll accept whatever is deemed suitable.' I take a deep breath, secretly dreading the thought of prison.

'Although.' Costello continues, this time stopping me by taking my arm. 'They might look in favour of your emotional state-'

'I'm not going to play on it. Yes what I did was for her, but no, I know I did wrong.'

'Ok.' He says simply. I go to walk away before I remember I need to tell him something.

'By the way, I quit the Fleet. I'm no longer Second.'

'You'd probably have gotten a dishonourable discharge anyway.' He replies after a moment of thought.

'Mummy, I want to play.' She wriggles from my arms and runs ahead holding my hand. We make our way into the craft and are met in the main seating room by Jake and Rigel, uncuffed. Jake jumps to his feet when he sees me and I can't wipe the smile from my face and go to hug him but a little girl clings to my trouser pocket, stopping me.

'You got her out!' Jake says surprised.

'Costello did.' I admit. 'Jake. Rigel. This is Lyra.' I try to step aside but she moves with me.

Jake and Rigel decide to take a step back and allow Lyra get use to them at a distance. Which it doesn't take her long to do. Within the hour she's playing catch with Jake, colouring with Rigel and colouring with me. All these things found out from the crafts emergency family cupboard, which gets used in the dire, and rare, cases that involves families. She spends the rest of the morning into early afternoon running around.

Watching Jake get on with Lyra and play games with her stirred something inside me. Watching them together filled me with a happiness that made me feel like I would burst with pride. Watching them I see a future play out before my eyes. I know he'd be a great dad. My heart races once more at them. The two people in the world that make me the happiness.

Then it dawns on me. I now know.

I ask Jake if I can talk to him in private. Lyra is now comfortable with Rigel. She's a confident little personality but I still tell her that I'll 'only be over there' if she'd needed me.

We step the other side of the door into a small hallway between the seating room and the cockpit with large windows on each side.

'Hey.' I say nervously.

'Hey.' He grins placing his hands on my waist, making me feel like a nervous teenager with her crush rather than two adults who are entering, what would have to be given the fact a child is involved, a mature relationship.

'So...' all my vocabulary have seemingly vanished. 'I saw the way you were with Lyra...' I paused finding my words.

'Yeah?' he gives me a big grin.

'And it made me realise something.'

'What's that?' he asked still grinning and making butterflies go crazy inside me.

'It made me see a future. I know we've got a long road yet before all this is over but...it made me see that...I love you.'

He grin vanishes as though he can't believe what I said before it reappears.

'You're sure?'

'Yes! 'I pull him in for a kiss wrapping my arms around his neck and he reciprocates by lifting me in the air as we kiss.

We re-enter the seating room side by side but not hand in hand. It's too soon to let Lyra know - not that I'd introduced him as my boyfriend or expect her to call him dad straight away. I'd allow her to do that in her own time.

I silently decide to ignore all the upcoming court dates and interrogation and focus on being with Lyra. I took her presence for granted before. Never again. Never will I ignore the fact that she could be gone so quick. For the rest of the journey we play hide and seek, tag and pretend to be animals while she rides on our backs.

Of course the inevitable happened. We were all interrogated. I admitted everything. How I was put on the case as a last resort because the simply was no one else to fill in on a plan I'd thought of. I told them how I hadn't planned to use Jake or Rigel, let alone tell them everything and have them willingly be part of finding Lyra. I admitted to how I felt I couldn't tell the Fleet my findings due to knowing I wouldn't be believed. I admitted that I stole files and weapons without consent. I even admitted how, in defence, I defended Jake and shot Rapha when he attacked.

Lyra began school late but she didn't seem to notice she was starting behind all her new school friends. In typical Lyra fashion she took it all in her stride and settled in quickly.

My armed healed eventually but I'll have 4 long scars for the rest of my life.

Jake lost his job at the Mechanics Sector. I feel that is my fault but he tells me he isn't that bothered by it. Luckily, my father decided to hire him as the Royal Mechanic, looking after our personal air crafts and various other mechanical transporters. My father says it's because he helped find his grandchild and that he was impressed with the craft he'd built from scratch. I don't personally care what his reason for hiring him is. He gets to live in the castle and I get to see him often.

Rigel was also offered a job but he turned it down. He said he was too use to living his own way. I told him he was welcome to visit at the castle anytime he wanted.

I increased the security around Lyra. Placed security outside her bedroom door and outside her balcony window where Rapha broke in.

Weeks later we went to court.

We heard the evidence against Rapha Blagden, how he'd held a grudge against Rigel for many years and had planned to frame him. It came out that in order to frame him and send him away for the rest of his life he had to think of a crime suitable, which was when he'd thought about targeting the royal family in order to make it happen. He makes me sick. He was sentenced to death for being too high a risk to society as well as his crimes.

Jake and Rigel were sentenced to two months' worth of community service for handling stolen information and weaponry. Rigel was also cleared of his outstanding crimes for helping find Lyra.

Me? I gave my version of events as honestly as I did in interrogation. Others gave their versions too. Costello, Jake, Rigel, my father. The judge was kind. He said he understood why I made the decisions that I did. Even mentioned my emotional state during that time even though I tried not to. He decided, given my title, it'd be safer for me to be put under house arrest for a year. I had a tag put on me and I'm not allowed to leave my front door or leave the premises. For a year. I'll get through it. I won't complain. I won't be able to take Lyra to school or pick her up. I'll find something to concentrate on. Maybe I'll focus on my duties and prepare to become Queen.

It'll be difficult but I don't care though. We're home.

Printed in the United States
By Bookmasters